Grace Notes

Grace Notes

Lorraine V. Murray

Resurrection Press
An Imprint of
CATHOLIC BOOK PUBLISHING CO.
Totowa • New Jersey

First published in March, 2002 by

    Catholic Book Publishing/Resurrection Press

    77 West End Road

    Totowa, NJ 07512

ISBN 1-878717-73-8 (h/c)

ISBN 1-878718-69-X (p/b)

Library of Congress Catalog Card Number: 2001-135974

Cover design and photo by John Murello

Printed in Canada

1 2 3 4 5 6 7 8 9

To Jef —

My sweetheart, friend, and husband

Contents

"For Christ plays in ten thousand places,
Lovely in limbs, and lovely in eyes not his
To the Father through the features of men's faces."

—*Gerard Manley Hopkins*

Acknowledgments

I am deeply grateful to my husband, Jef, who is always my first reader and who provides honest, thoughtful, and compassionate feedback; my spiritual director, Monsignor Richard Lopez, for his insights and prayers; the children in my life, especially Stephen, Sarah, and Isabelle, whose stories appear on these pages; and Emilie Cerar of Resurrection Press for her faith in me and for all her hard work.

I am also grateful to the editors of the following publications, in which versions of many chapters of this book were originally published, including:

"A Child's Eyes," which appeared as "Spiritual Insights Abound in Most Ordinary Places," *The Atlanta Journal-Constitution*, May 6, 2000.

"Place of Faith," *America*, June 17-24, 2000.

"Don Juan and Friends," which appeared as "Faith in a Rose," *America*, August 27-September 3, 2001.

"A Deeper Chord," which appeared as "Marriage Vows Now Strike a Deeper Chord," *The Georgia Bulletin*, February 8, 2001.

"The Journey," which appeared as "Journey Is Over: Put in a Good Word for Me with the Lord," *The Atlanta Journal-Constitution*, November 11, 2000.

"Waking Up," which appeared as "Cancer Battle Offers Lessons About Love," *The Atlanta Journal-Constitution*, July 22, 2000.

"Turning Doris," which appeared as "Embracing Christ First," *America*, April 22, 2000.

"No Vacancy for Satan," which appeared as "Hang Up No Vacancy Sign for Prince of Darkness," *The Atlanta Journal-Constitution*, October 7, 2000.

"Mother Teresa and the Manatees," which appeared as "My First Miracle," in *Sacred Journey,* Vol. 40, No. 4, August, 1999.

"Little Ways," which appeared as "Often, Small Acts of Love Mean the Most," *The Atlanta Journal-Constitution,* December 16, 2000.

"Trio of Love Notes, *America,* March 19, 2001.

"Valentine for God," which appeared as "Consider Sending God a Valentine Message," *The Georgia Bulletin,* February. 15, 2001.

"Voices of Silence," which appeared as "How Can We Know What God's Voice Sounds Like?" *The Atlanta Journal-Constitution,* April 8, 2000.

"Heart Whispers," which appeared as "Heeding His Voice," *America,* March 12, 2001.

"World Out of Orbit," which appeared as "Medical News Can Upend a Life," *The Atlanta Journal-Constitution,* May 20, 2000.

"Change of Heart," *America,* February 26, 2001.

"Jack in the Box God," which appeared as "Attacks Weren't God's Vengeance," *The Atlanta Journal-Constitution,* September 22, 2001.

"His Trespasses," which appeared as "A Fierce Love," *America,* June 4-11, 2001.

"Least of These," *America,* January 22-29, 2001.

"Simplifying," which appeared as "Feeding His Sheep," *America,* July 15-22, 2000.

"Gospel of Consumerism," which appeared as "Gospel of Consumerism Ultimately Will Betray Us," *The Atlanta Journal-Constitution,* July 14, 2000.

"Kingdom Called 'Enough,'" *The Georgia Bulletin,* September, 2001.

Foreword

I stood at the bedside of a hospitalized friend, a giant of a man laid low by a heart attack. He is closer to my husband than a brother and, unlike an infrequently seen relative, this one is impossible to ignore and regularly present. Made up of two parts visionary and one part bull, when he succeeds, the world changes, and when he fails, many lives shake. Over two decades, we held on to love through many upheavals and times of truth telling. The last time we'd spoken, our evening at a lovely restaurant had ended with me flailing my hands in disbelief and saying, "What did you expect?" One of his grand ideas had left someone else to walk through fire.

Now he'd been leveled. Several people were in the room when he called me over, waving a copy of *Sacred Journey*, the journal I edit that had been given him as good "bedridden" reading. "Do you have anything in here that tells you what to do when you get off the bus, thinking it's where God has told you to go, and he's nowhere to be found?" he asked. I said, "Perhaps God is wearing a different disguise than you expected. Keep looking." He was hoping for a God of instant miracles, and that God wasn't stopping by.

Several days later the manuscript for *Grace Notes* arrived and I did what I always do when something new arrives from Lorraine V. Murray. Whether it's a new article for me to review or an email to answer or a full-length book, I don't delay. Lorraine never wastes my time—she always has something consequential to say. So I propped my feet up and began to read. First one story, then another were dog-eared—balm for me—and marked as good medicine for my friend. Here in "Fearful Encounters" was a message he needed to hear. Underneath all those fears of abandonment, suffering, and dying, lay another deeper worry: What if the promises of Christ are false? What if when you die you will confront total nothingness? What if you get off the bus and God isn't there?

That's when prayer steps in. I'd told my friend that day in the hospital that his job was to keep looking around at the bus stop while he let his body heal. Our job as his friends was to keep praying. We'd keep him propped up when he couldn't muster much faith or hope. When Lorraine faced down her own fears during an illness, she found a friend in prayer who said: "I stand for all the prayers that have been said for you during the past year, and all the prayers being said for you by your friends, your church community, your family, your readers." When we grab the hand of this power called prayer, fears, even the most ferocious ones, will be resized.

So, lucky readers, it's your turn to listen for the grace notes, those sweet, melancholy sounds that can be heard by a well-tuned heart. Lorraine's is like that. She's been listening and recording what she's heard. As you read, you'll begin to recognize—as I did— that she's saying just what you have been longing to hear.

—*Rebecca Laird*

Rebecca Laird is the editor of *Sacred Journey: The Journal of Fellowship in Prayer,* an interfaith spirituality publication based in Princeton, NJ.

Introduction

The book you hold in your hands is the result of countless cups of coffee, numerous prayers, a few tears, and many chocolates.

I named it *Grace Notes* because Grace is a family name that I share with my mom, who was Grace Mary Bibbo, and my niece, Jennifer Grace, and because the essays record many little revelations of God's love in my everyday life.

In music, grace notes are short, delicate touches embellishing the more prominent notes of a melody. Grace notes suggest lightness, sweetness, gentleness, and often playfulness—but they also decorate music with a melancholy edge.

This description seems to sum up my life thus far. Plenty of sweet and gentle moments, plenty of playfulness—and plenty of sadness.

In February of 1999, I quit a life-sapping job in university publications to become a free-lance writer. The months since then have been the happiest—and saddest—of my life.

God has generously blessed my efforts to become a writer. I have to pinch myself to be sure I'm awake when I see my byline in the "Faith and Values" section of *The Atlanta-Journal Constitution*. Another pinch when I see my mug shot in the national magazine *America*. And a really big pinch when I see my articles on the web site of the American Cancer Society.

I feel as though I'm split into two distinct people. One is the confident and serene lady who writes about spiritual issues, the lady who seems graced with a deep faith.

But I'm all too familiar with the other lady. She is a very ordinary, high-anxiety person who slouches around the house in her cow-pattern pajamas. She's the one who quakes in fear over the prospect of getting a mammogram. She is a connoisseur of worrying.

When I told a priest about my "two-lady" theory, he suggested that I go back and re-read the many articles I'd written over the years.

"God is sending you grace through your writing to help you face the difficulties in your life," he said.

As I was following his advice, I received a letter from Emilie Cerar at Resurrection Press. She had seen my articles in *America* and wondered if I might be interested in writing a book.

Had I received Emilie's letter only a few months earlier, I would have danced around the house with glee. Ever since my days as a little chubby child growing up in Miami, I had dreamed of writing a book. However, on the day her letter arrived, I was exhausted and depressed. I threw the letter on my desk without emitting even one chirp of joy.

I was in the middle of seven weeks of daily radiation-therapy treatments for breast cancer, which had been diagnosed in May of 2000. My two ladies had very different reactions to the prospect of writing a book. One was excited about having a lifelong dream come true. But the other lady, weary and dejected, had a stronger voice. And so I didn't look at the letter for another month.

When I finally began to emerge from the "Oh, no, this can't be happening to me!" stage of my illness, I called Emilie. Her first remark was, "I was just thinking about you. I'm sitting here reading one of your articles in *America*!" The timing of that phone call chased away any initial doubts I might have had about starting the project.

Still, there were times when I doubted myself. Times when I wondered if I had the necessary drive to tackle such a huge project. Gradually, however, as the months have passed, I've come to believe this book is part of God's big mysterious plan for my life, just like my illness is.

The book has eleven sections, which are the little sign-posts of my faith journey. The categories—believing, trusting, praying, suffering, forgiving, simplifying, resurrection, serving, denying, grace, and loving—are not rigid and they are not arranged chronologically. Praying and trusting often overlap, as do believing and serving. Denying God seems to happen over and over, even in the midst of loving Him.

The essays were born of my desire to know Christ in a more heartfelt way. I longed to dance with Him at a wedding and weep with Him in the garden. I wanted to know the gentle man who loved fishing, eating with His friends, and praying in the desert. I wanted to know the man who invited His friends to a feast He prepared by shouting: "Come and have breakfast . . ." (John 21:12).

And I yearned to explore a question that had hounded me for years. Why did Christ come to Earth? Why did He show up in our broken world?

When I was a child, the nuns told me He came to die for our sins. He came to open the gates of heaven. I realize this answer is one thread in the complex tapestry of standard Christian theology, but maybe I'm just too dumb to get it. When I try to mesh the concepts of original sin, the opening of the heavenly gates, and Jesus' death on the cross, I come face to face with a bloodthirsty God demanding that His beloved son die the most horrible, agonizing death imaginable.

Maybe the whole thing is much more simple.

I think Christ came to teach us the hard lessons about loving and living—and about dying.

Christ fully immersed himself in our broken world. He loved people who were flawed. They were harlots, tax collectors, and thieves. He loved people that others feared, the lepers and the demon-possessed. Instead of shooing away little kids, He hugged them. Instead of condemning His torturers, He forgave them. His love didn't entail big emotional outbursts or passionate proclamations. He loved by serving, by washing His friends' feet and by healing those who were desperate and abandoned.

In the 33 years He walked among us, Christ turned the whole world upside down. He told us the poor are rich, the last are first, the meek are blessed, and the dead are alive. Trying to follow His path can seem frustrating—and impossible at times—especially when we feel like we're tripping over every pebble—and boulder—on the way. But, even when we fall into a pit of doubt and sin, He reaches out a hand and lifts us back up.

To grasp His insights about dying, we must first acknowledge what seems impossible: the bitter fact of our own mortality. Whether we live to be 20, 60, or 100, we all eventually will have to "check out" of this big earthly hotel. When we are 20, we imagine ourselves calmly accepting death at age 60. But when we are

60, we long to be 70, and when we are 80, we are still not ready to pack our bags and exit gracefully.

Christ didn't walk to His death in a calm, resigned manner. He prayed and wept, and pleaded with God on the night before the crucifixion. He begged His friends to pray with Him. He described His emotional state in dramatic terms: "sorrowful until death."

If Christ's story had ended on the cross, it would have been tragic indeed. But we know the final chapter of Christ's mission was the resurrection. Agony gave way to bliss, and groans became laughter.

A lovely prayer by Cardinal Newman in *The Catholic Prayer Book* eloquently captures the idea that, like Jesus, we all have a mission to complete:

> May the Lord support us all the day long, until the shades lengthen and the evening comes, and the busy world is hushed, and the fever of life is over, and our work is done. Then in His mercy may He grant us safe lodging, a holy rest, and peace at last.

This book is my effort to do the work the Lord has given me. It is my attempt to convey the small illuminations that reveal His presence in my everyday life. Whether I'm volunteering in a nursing home, playing with my goddaughter, anguishing over my illness, or clipping roses in my garden, it seems I encounter Christ everywhere.

I pray this book will give you insights into the ordinary moments that reveal Christ's grace in your life. I pray that it will sustain you in bitter moments of sorrow and pain.

And I pray this book will help you encounter God everywhere. In the garden, in the kitchen, in the chapel, in the cradle, on the road. In the face of your beloved, and in your very own heart. Over and over. Everywhere.

I

Believing

As a little child, my faith in God, in Christ, in the Catholic Church, arose in my heart as naturally and easily as my certainty that the sun would rise the next day. Faith was in the water I drank, in the cereal I ate. I buttered my bread with faith. I sipped its sweetness in cups of hot chocolate.

I felt faith in my fingertips as they slid over the crystal rosary beads that draped from my hands in church. I inhaled the spicy scent of faith in the incense that burned at Mass. I tasted faith on my tongue, when I opened my mouth to receive the body of Christ, a substance so sacred that even grazing it with the teeth was sacrilegious.

In my eyes, the whole world was Catholic. I was born in Yonkers, N.Y., into a family that traced its Catholic roots back in time for many generations. Although my parents were native New Yorkers, their parents hailed from Sicily and Naples.

I thought everyone ate fish on Friday, went to confession on Saturday and Mass on Sunday. I thought everyone recognized the different landscapes of venial and mortal sins. I thought everyone's life was encircled by the same boundaries.

When I was seven, my family migrated to Miami. There, we lived in a little turquoise house, with a yard embroidered with palm trees and gaudy tropical flowers. In the heavy summer heat, the towering trees sagged under the weight of coconuts, banana trees grew pregnant with tiny green fingers, and little shy lizards with crimson throats zipped across our patio.

When I went to church and knelt to pray in front of the tabernacle, I took comfort in remembering what the nuns had told me. God was hidden there, disguised as bread. I took comfort in the ritual of the Mass, which was as predictable as hibiscus buds exploding into bloom or mangos turning from green to tawny yellow.

I tiptoed close to the mystery that was God when I repeated the ponderous Latin phrases that I'd learned in catechism class.

"Dominus vobiscum," the priest intoned at the start of Mass, and our reply was always the same: *"Et cum spiritu tuo."*

I didn't understand why we spoke Latin at Mass. I didn't understand how the bread and wine became Christ's flesh and blood. Nor did I understand how birds sang or how lizards changed colors. Accepting the existence of a hidden realm beyond my grasp, I felt life bristled with things I would never understand. But God was the blood that surged through the veins of the universe. He had everything under control. That was my faith.

In high school religion class, the nuns told us about people who were "fallen away" Catholics, but I never met one until I went to college and became one myself. When I "fell away" from the faith, however, I didn't experience any immediate bruises. Instead, I felt very free as I proudly turned my back on years of religious training and the church's seemingly endless list of rules.

In philosophy class, I pored over books by atheists like Karl Marx and Jean-Paul Sartre. Stunned by their brilliance, I bowed to their conclusions about the world and embraced atheism with the fervor I'd once showered on the saints. As I revised the boundaries of my life, venial and mortal sins became dusty relics of my past. I felt it didn't matter whether I drank too much or partied too wildly. The rules could always be adjusted to suit my inclinations. Everything was relative.

Returning to Catholicism many years later, I discovered something about faith that my childhood catechism hadn't mentioned. Paradoxically enough, the long dry spell of disbelief had produced a robust harvest. I was able to observe the rituals of my religion with fresh eyes and hear the words of scripture with fresh ears.

I was especially thrilled by the story of the Good Shepherd, who was restless and disheartened when even one of His lambs was missing. I pictured myself as a lamb that had wandered far away from Christ for many years and envisioned Christ gently coaxing me to His side. I saw myself nestled against Him as He carried me back to a safe enclosure.

I felt lifted up. I felt rescued. I felt I was reclaiming the place of my childhood faith. And in coming full circle, I believe I've come to terms with my childhood's boundaries. I see now that the boundaries were, all along, not restricting me but protecting me.

Today, in a mysterious way, they also embrace me. This makes perfect sense, given what else I've discovered. The boundaries are, in the end, nothing less than the loving arms of Jesus Christ.

1

❀ A Child's Eyes ❀

One morning, I was having breakfast with my best friend, Pam, and her family. Munching on an orange slice, her small son, Stephen, extracted a seed and held it up triumphantly.

"I'm going to plant this seed," he declared joyfully, "and grow an orange tree."

His mother and I paused from our coffee to smile. His grandmother and great-grandmother nodded appreciatively. None of us had the heart to point out that Atlanta's climate isn't tropical enough for an orange tree to thrive.

Stephen is only five-and-a-half years old—and for him, the world is a place of boundless wonders. In his kitchen at home, he's created a nature window crowded with treasures—feathers, acorns, rocks, and shells gathered from a lake, the seaside, and his own backyard.

On his porch, a bucket teems with tadpoles that he and his dad rescued from a bull-dozed pond. Stephen checks them each day, eagerly awaiting their transformation into frogs.

I often envy the faith of small boys like Stephen. We grown-ups tend to water down faith with ponderous dogmas, rituals, and sermons. We somberly seek God in churches, mosques, temples, and monasteries. Too often we discover a rather anemic version of the divine, a weary CEO in the sky.

Maybe, if we could see the world through a child's eyes, we might embrace a truly living faith—a faith glowing with red-hot fire in its veins.

Stephen wraps his arms around life's wonders daily. Anything is possible on a planet where homely caterpillars sprout into butterflies and festive tulips stubbornly emerge through the crusty earth each spring.

Sleepwalking through life, adults so often miss the obvious. Checking my garden one morning, I congratulated myself on the plump, ruby tips crowning each rose bush. Feeling somewhat smug, I started heading back inside the house, and it was only by accident that I saw what was really there. Clinging to each bud were herds of tiny green, and no doubt hungry, caterpillars.

"Religion is really about seeing," writes Richard Rohr in his book *Everything Belongs*. "Buddha" means "I am awake," he points out, and in Zen Buddhism, a state of awareness called "beginner's mind" gives people fresh lenses to see the world.

Christ came to rouse us from our spiritual slumber. Described in St. John's gospel as the "light of the world," Christ urged people to struggle against the darkness. He gave sight to the blind and reminded us that if our eyes were healthy, we'd be "full of light."

In the gospels, people sometimes "saw" Christ but failed to recognize Him. After the crucifixion, Mary Magdalene mistook Him for the gardener at the tomb. When Jesus appeared to the disciples on the road to Emmaus, they didn't realize who He was. Only when He blessed and broke the bread were their eyes opened.

You don't have to teach children about seeing, of course. Send a boy like Stephen out to the backyard and he'll unearth a tangle of fine worms. Send him to the lake and he'll retrieve a festive sala-mander or two. An inchworm discovered in the garden can become a pet for an hour or so. His day is one long hosanna to God's creation.

Unfortunately, that lovely celebration of the world often evades grown-ups. Although I've lived on the same block for 17 years and take a walk every day, I don't think I could describe from memo-ry the color of each house or the flowerbeds in each yard. Immersed in my worries about the future and my regrets over the past, I miss the glories of the here and now.

Christ urged us to become childlike to enter the kingdom of heaven. And He filled his parables with fish, trees, lilies, seeds, grapes, sparrows, and lambs. Ordinary, down-to-earth things kids know well. Things that wake us up to the full-blooded present moment.

Christ knew how precious a child's faith is. And how limitless. I doubt that Christ would discourage a small boy from planting an orange seed. Nor would He be surprised to see that seed springing to life in a sunny corner of the boy's room.

2

❀ Place of Faith ❀

I stepped gingerly into the room. It was only my third week volunteering at the nursing home, and I was still unsure of myself.

A curtain enclosed the bed near the window. A small fan lazily moved its head back and forth, stirring the air and muffling all sounds. I gently pushed aside the curtain, and peeked inside.

I was transfixed by what I saw.

The woman, fast asleep, looked just like my mother. She had the same smooth olive skin and heart-shaped face. The thin wisps of molasses-brown hair that slipped from a flowery scarf on her head were the same color.

My eyes pooled with hot tears. I stood for a moment, drinking in the sight, and then tiptoed from the room.

My mother had died of cancer when I was 29. Although I'd fancied myself an atheist at the time, I'd made a secret pact with God when she had first become ill: "If you cure her, I will return to my faith." After her death, I'd returned to atheism with all the ardor I'd once bestowed on Catholicism.

Eventually, I surrendered my grudge against God and started groping my way back to my childhood faith. I was in my forties when I made an appointment to speak with the pastor of a Catholic church in downtown Decatur, just a mile from my home.

Sitting on an overstuffed armchair in the rectory, I somewhat nervously described my humble stirring of belief.

"It's just a tiny seed," I admitted.

The priest smiled broadly and assured me it was enough.

I tended to the little seed by dutifully attending Mass and saying my prayers, hoping that old habits might uproot my residual weeds of doubt. Did I truly embrace the Church's teachings after so many years of atheism? Did I really accept the consecrated bread and wine as Christ's body and blood? Did I believe in Christ's divinity? At first, my truthful answer was, "No, not really."

But I desperately wanted to believe. I longed for the certainty I'd once had in childhood. I longed for the comfort that came from the sacraments. And I hoped my little seed would one day erupt into a green and vibrant faith.

Hoping to jumpstart the whole faith process, I threw myself into volunteer work. After all, if I was going to give Christianity a second try, I didn't want to stand on the sidelines. It was my duties as a minister to the sick that had brought me to the nursing home, where I took Holy Communion to an elderly woman each week.

One day, in the lobby of the nursing home, I met two Cuban sisters who were visiting their mother. Their dark hair and eyes reminded me of my Italian-American heritage. When I said that I'd enjoy meeting their mom some time, the sisters smiled. She was recovering from an operation and would welcome a visit, they assured me.

It was their mother, fast asleep, whom I saw that day. Afterwards, I rushed home to share the news with my husband, Jef.

"She looks so much like my mom, it's uncanny," I said breathlessly. "I can't wait to go back and talk with her."

A few days later, I returned to the nursing home and walked quickly to her room. I was nervous. What if she weren't there any more? What if something had happened to her?

My hands were trembling when I approached the door. Inside, the same fan stirred the steamy summer air. But this time the curtain was drawn back. The woman, wearing a bright turquoise housecoat and a flowery scarf on her hair, was sitting up in bed. She gave me a big smile and, using a mixture of English and Spanish, welcomed me into the room.

I stood there, dumbfounded, trying to make sense of the scene. She was a beautiful woman, there was no doubt—and she was the same woman I'd seen a few days ago.

But she bore no resemblance at all to my mother.

It was only later that I realized what had happened. So many times since my mother's death, I had yearned for the feel of her hand on my brow, the music of her laughter on the phone. More times than I can count, I had longed to travel backwards in time, to arrive in her hospital room as she lay dying.

I wanted to have a final conversation with her. To tell her I'd never forget her and that I loved her as much as it's possible for one person to love another. But as the years had passed, I'd learned to content myself with occasional sightings of her in my dreams.

In one dream, we'd sat across from one another at my kitchen table. I'd grasped her hand and told her how much I loved her.

"Please, Mommy, won't you come back to me?" I'd pleaded.

With infinite tenderness, she'd smiled at me and said softly, "I can't."

In her own way, though, she had come back to me, just for a few moments, in the nursing home.

What did it all mean, I wondered. My rational mind balked at mystical interpretations, but in my heart I felt sure of what I had seen. Finally, my heart won out over my skepticism as I endeavored to preserve the treasure God had given me.

My mother, I felt sure, had sent me a message. I believe she was telling me that she was, in some mysterious way, still with me. That she'd always be hidden in the lined and weary faces of the ailing and elderly people I visited.

And she wanted to tell me that, no matter how often I might stumble, I would in the end arrive at a green and thriving realm. A place my mother had never left. A place of faith.

3

 Don Juan and Friends

When I walk into the side garden and spot my three rosebushes, their branches tangling merrily in the wind, I'm reminded of how precious everyday faith is. Especially faith in our own capabilities and in renewal. And faith in doubtful outcomes.

When my husband and I first moved into our home in Decatur 17 years ago, I yearned to raise roses, but I kept facing mental roadblocks. In my estimation, roses were magical beings that only cleverer women could produce. Women who wore crisp cotton sundresses and were surrounded by little gaggles of smiling children. Women who were, first and foremost, nurturers.

Childless, I've often suspected that the nurturing gene somehow passed me by. I've never been adept at the homey undertakings other women take for granted, like selecting just the right wallpaper for the kitchen, putting dust ruffles on the beds, and knowing the exact angle you hold a baby to produce a hearty burp.

As the years passed, my yearning to grow roses didn't diminish, but every time I was tempted, I reminded myself sternly that my thumb lacked even the slightest smudge of green. Besides, I told myself, our side garden is too shaded, and roses need sunlight to thrive. I tried to content myself with admiring the roses grown by other women in the neighborhood.

One white rosebush decorating my neighbor's yard particularly captured my fancy. Every time I walked by, I stopped to marvel at the miniature blooms, which were as delicate as seashells.

One day in a local nursery, I spotted two young rosebushes sitting side by side in containers. They were tagged "Joseph's Coat" and "Don Juan." As I gazed longingly at the pictures on the tags, I envisioned myself in my garden, cutting a cluster of roses in the spring. On an impulse, I decided to take a chance. I bought the two bushes and loaded them into my car.

A few days later, I was running a high fever. My body was covered with itchy red welts. After the doctor confirmed my suspicion that I'd come down with chicken pox, I was housebound for a few weeks. As I was regaining my strength, I'd sit on the front porch swing and admire the rosebushes that were still in their containers a few yards away. Somehow, just looking at them gave me hope.

Despite the fact that I shuddered when I saw my reflection in the mirror, I told myself that maybe I'd get well, maybe I'd plant those bushes—and maybe they'd produce some stunning roses.

That was five years ago. I did get well, I planted the bushes, and much to my surprise, they have been thriving ever since. Despite the meager amount of sunlight in the garden, each spring Joseph's Coat bursts into a crazy quilt of red, orange, and yellow flowers, while Don Juan sports a cloak of velvety red blooms. For most of spring and summer, the vase on my dining room table never lacks a long-stemmed occupant.

A year ago, Joseph and Don welcomed a new friend. One day, Jef and I saw our neighbors revamping their front lawn. A closer inspection revealed they had uprooted the little bush I'd admired so much and tossed it upon the trash heap. Ever so carefully, we retrieved the bedraggled bush, carried it home, and planted it near the other roses. After a few days of dutiful watering, my reward was the sight of green nubs emerging on its branches. That spring, a cluster of tiny white roses added their voices to the symphony of color in the side garden.

Still, I don't congratulate myself that somehow I've managed to do everything right. The truth is the roses seem to be doing fine without me. Of course, I water them during dry spells and prune them in the winter, but that's about it. They seem to have minds of their own. Slowly they are taking over the side garden, sinking deeper roots and sending out fingers that creep up the side of the house.

Even in winter, when they are leafless, brown, and rather forlorn looking, the trio of rosebushes reminds me of the everyday miracles in my life. People, I've learned, do survive terrible ailments. Women like me who are clumsy around children can somehow keep roses alive. And even a rosebush that was thrown away can make a comeback. What wonders we can witness if we just have faith.

Questions for Reflection and Discussion

1. What childhood memories of prayer and worship are the grounds of your religious experience today?

2. Peering through the lens of faith, revisit a departed loved one's last conversation with you and share your experience.

3. What are some everyday miracles your faith helps you witness?

II

Trusting

In our living room sits an antique rocking chair, which looks harmless enough—but don't let it fool you.

Inherited from my husband's grandmother, Gladys Lester, it is a handsome walnut chair with a wicker back and seat. When you plop down, it tilts backward at a very precarious angle, giving you the impression you're about to flip over onto your head.

Over the years, I've used the chair as a litmus test for people visiting our home for the first time. If a guest melts into the chair and seems unfazed by the odd angle it assumes, I peg the person as secure and trusting. When some poor soul springs from the chair as if a demon had materialized in the living room, I know we're kindred spirits.

Something deep inside me refuses to let go and trust the chair. Even though I have plenty of evidence that the chair will not tip over, a little place in my stomach clutches in fear whenever I give it a try.

The chair reminds me of my difficulties in trusting God. Even though Christ told His disciples numerous times not to fret over the morrow and not to be afraid, still I have trouble trusting in divine providence.

As a child, I assumed that trusting God meant striking a deal with Him. "OK, God, I'll trust you," I was in effect saying, "as long as that means things will turn out the way I want them to. I'll trust you to shield me from disappointment and suffering."

Gradually I've come to suspect the truth. Trusting God is no guarantee against heartache and pain. Trusting God does not spare us from aging, illness, accidents, or death. Instead, trust means acknowledging that He loves us and wants what's best for us. As St. Paul so beautifully stated it: "We know that all things work together for good for those who love God" (Romans 8:28).

Although there's no blueprint for surrendering our doubts and fears, it helps to remember we are children in God's eyes. We are all tiny babes looking to Him for tenderness and care. As a Father, He will watch over us.

But even God's beloved child, Christ, was not spared from suffering, and in the final days of His life, He gave us a model for confronting our own suffering and death. He could have run away. He could have fought against His accusers. But He knew His suffering would not be in vain.

In the Garden of Gethsemane, He showed us that it is not shameful to cry. It is not shameful to plead with God.

He also showed us the real meaning of trust, when He accepted the cup of pain that His father gave Him. Like Christ, we must pick up our cross, dust it off, and stumble down the path God has earmarked for us. Even though we are squinting "through a glass darkly," as St. Paul said, and we aren't sure of our destination, we still must follow the path.

Do I fully trust God? I'd be lying if I told you I did. But I am working on it, just like I'm working on someday plopping down in the rocking chair—and enjoying the ride.

4

❖ A Deeper Chord ❖

Most women don't marry the same man twice, unless they've had second thoughts after a divorce.

I'm an exception, however. I've stood before the altar and pronounced my vows to the same man on two separate occasions—and I'm pleased to say we've never divorced.

When Jef and I married on June 12, 1982, neither of us were churchgoers. Still, we had been raised in Christian households and craved the standard trimmings for our wedding—stained glass windows, oak pews, and an altar. Without much concern about denominations, we chose the Druid Hills Methodist Church, which was near my apartment in Atlanta.

The church had a lovely sanctuary and a kind minister, the Rev. Warren Harbert, who didn't seem ruffled by our wishy-washy feelings about religion. Maybe, on some level, he suspected that our choice of a setting was not as arbitrary as we thought. Perhaps he knew that our presence in the church was an example of the mysterious ways that Christ nudges His lambs back into the fold.

Jef and I agreed to stick by each other "for better or worse, for richer or poorer, in sickness and in health." But as I stood there in my crisp veil and frothy white gown with seed pearls on the bodice, I couldn't imagine hard times or illness. After all, we were young, healthy, and reasonably well-heeled.

The words "until death do us part" brought an unexpected rush of tears to my eyes. I did not want the specter of death to haunt us on that lovely summer day.

"Nothing will ever part us," I thought fiercely.

Our lives followed a fairly predictable pattern for well-educated, upwardly mobile couples. We followed Jef's job to the Washington, D.C. area, where we lived for two years. We bought a townhouse, a TV, a VCR, and a couch. We adopted a cat, a white fellow with a black spot on his back that looked like Africa. We named him "Chunk." Jef worked as an electrical engineer, while I taught philosophy and English at the University of D.C. and Northern Virginia Community College.

We were homesick, though, for the South, and in 1984 we moved to Decatur, just a few miles from my old apartment.

When I returned to Catholicism, we had a rude awakening. We discovered the Church didn't recognize our marriage. Since I was a "cradle Catholic," our failure to get married by a Catholic priest was, well, not kosher. Wanting to cross all the t's and dot all the i's just right, we arranged to marry again, this time in the Catholic Church. It was fun planning a second reception and ordering the same decadent chocolate cake that we'd had at our first wedding.

And so we married again, this time at St. Thomas More Catholic Church, which was about a mile from our home in Decatur. On Valentine's Day of 1993, we stood before our beloved pastor, the Rev. Pat Mulhern, and repeated the same vows from so many years before.

This time, though, the vows struck a much deeper chord—maybe because we had so much more mileage on our hearts.

The words "for better or worse" brought a little smile to my lips. When we'd first set up our home together, I'd promised myself that Jef would never see me in rollers. And I would never, under any circumstances, slouch around the house in a comfy, shapeless bathrobe and fuzzy slippers.

Over the years, the rules had relaxed considerably.

We had seen each other despondent, angry, worried, tipsy, and ecstatic. We'd laughed, cried, and prayed together. On more than one occasion, he had glimpsed me in my robe and furry slippers, with my hair in rollers. But he seemed unperturbed.

The "richer or poorer" vow had also taken on a new twist.

Although we'd embarked on married life merrily digging ourselves into debt, it wasn't long before we began rethinking our habits. We certainly hadn't taken vows of poverty, but we had downscaled mightily. Jef eventually left the hectic world of engineering and I fled the chaotic scene of university publications. Today, the car we drive is not snazzy and our sofa is tattered. But we are happier.

The vow about sickness and health really hit home. Over the years, we'd plied each other with cough medicine and chicken soup during flu season. He'd cared for me when I came down with pneumonia and then, shortly after, chicken pox. And I'd prayed fervently when a mysterious back ailment had kept him in constant pain for over a year.

"Until death do us part" again brought tears to my eyes. The strands of our lives had become so interwoven, it was hard to imagine one of us without the other. He cooked the appetizers and entrees; I baked the rolls and desserts. He painted; I wrote. He patched the roof; I mopped the floors.

Still, as we stood at the altar for the second time, death seemed elusive. It was something that happens when you're 90 or so.

"No need to think about it," I assured myself.

A few years later, when the Grim Reaper almost paid us a house call, I realized I could no longer avoid the phrase "until death do us part." But no matter how much I wept and fretted over my illness, Jef remained steady. Through his tenderness and compassion, he revealed Christ's loving presence in my life.

I was fortunate that my cancer was diagnosed early enough for treatment. But I still sometimes wonder what might happen if I were to die before Jef. Would he remember to dust the bookshelves? Prune the roses? Feed our pet gerbil? Would he be lonely?

And then I have to remind myself that someone bigger than both of us is steering our lifeboat. He is the one who calmed the sea. The one who helped the newlyweds at Cana. The one who said, over and over, "Fear not."

I am trying to follow His tender advice. I am trying to trust that God will take care of us, as He always has. During the good days and the bad, the rich times and the poor, in sickness and in health. Until the very end—and beyond.

5

 ## The Elephants' Tango

I went to visit my friend Isabelle the other afternoon. All smiles, she kissed me, grabbed a slice of bread and rushed into the yard.

Before I could stop her, Isabelle was on her back, hurling tidbits of bread at the sky.

"Isabelle," I cried, "What are you doing?"

"Feeding the birds," she chortled, as the crumbs rained upon her.

I had to laugh. Really, what could I expect? Isabelle is only three years old.

Still, despite her tender age, she is much more than a friend. She is also my teacher.

You see, I've long been intrigued by Christ's reminder that we can't enter the kingdom of heaven unless we become like little children. And as I've examined the holy books, I've noticed similar advice pouring from the lips of the Zen masters and the Christian saints.

Buddhists call it enlightenment. Christians call it the heavenly kingdom. And they agree that you can't enter these magical realms with the heavy, serious gait of an adult. You have to step lightly and freely. You have to imitate the heart of a child.

This advice seems impossible at first blush. Especially for someone like me who doesn't have kids. Might as well try to imitate a frog as a child.

But that's where Isabelle enters the picture.

One afternoon, my little teacher and I went for a stroll. Spotting a bright batch of pansies, she gently stroked their velvety heads. And then, before I could stop her, she ripped two flowers from their stalks and tucked them behind her ears.

I was tempted to reprimand her. Tempted to impart a homespun lesson about the necessity of looking rather than touching.

But Isabelle was smiling so radiantly I stopped myself. I tried to recall the last time I'd acted spontaneously. Without consulting my DayTimer or to-do list.

Moments later, Isabelle plopped down in the shade and upended a burlap sack filled with a menagerie of plastic animals. Under her watchful eye, toy elephants tangoed, horses sang, and zebras flew.

I sat down beside her. Suddenly I remembered spending hours playing "horses and men" as a child. But now the plastic horse lay lifeless in my hand. When had the miracle run dry?

We adults search for miracles in temples, churches, and mosques. Isabelle smiles at a butterfly and God smiles back.

We know Christ told His disciples over and over, "Fear not." But we run ourselves ragged trying to squelch our seemingly endless fears.

We install elaborate security systems in our homes and glaring lights in our yards. And still we are fearful. Fattening our IRAs and savings accounts, we try to nail down the future. But secretly we fear we'll never have enough.

Isabelle, like any child, has her share of imaginary fears, but she knows her father's hug can banish a battalion of leering monsters from beneath the bed.

One day, I went to the grocery store with Isabelle and her mom, Thadria.

"Be careful," Thadria admonished the child as we crossed a busy street. "The cars are dangerous."

Isabelle paused for a moment and then reached for her mother's outstretched hand. She smiled.

Maybe I shouldn't worry about Isabelle, but I do. At some point, she'll head to school, where she'll have to sit properly, one ankle crossed over the other. If she squirms, she'll be reprimanded and if she giggles out of turn, she'll be hushed.

Before long, she'll cross the border into adulthood. The zebras will stop flying and the horses will grow mute. And one day she may awaken from a long dreamless sleep to find herself like me, trying to imitate the heart of a child.

I hope she'll remember the day she threw bread at the sky. The day she wore pansies in her hair. I hope she'll remember her friend who visited her now and again. The lady who marveled at Isabelle's world. And took notes. The lady who realized that being childlike is the hardest thing in the world—and also the easiest.

You have to leave your DayTimer at home once in a while. Enjoy the snazzy flowers waving on green stalks. Treat the birds to a feast.

Laugh when things are funny. Cry when things are sad. And, above all, trust that someone much bigger than you has everything under control.

Questions for Reflection and Discussion

1. Is there some object, like the rocking chair, that reveals your degree of trust or mistrust?

2. What incidents have tested your trust in divine providence?

3. How can you learn to trust God more?

III

Praying

When the alarm clock bleats at 6 a.m. on weekdays, the ritual is predictable enough. After a quick bathroom trip, I head to the kitchen to brew a pot of coffee. Then I open the front door to catch a few notes from the daybreak bird choir, which, in the warmer months, stars robins, Carolina wrens, and mockingbirds.

Then it's back to bed for 20 minutes—but not to sleep.

I sit with my back propped comfortably against the pillows, within sight of my favorite stuffed animal, a fat cat named the Venerable St. Chunk. Trying to still my train of thoughts with the mantra, "love" or "Jesus," I spend quiet time with God before the busy day unfolds.

Morning prayer continues when I walk outside into our yard crowded with oak and pine trees, blueberry bushes, grape vines, and, in summer, a garden filled with tomatoes and eggplants. I sometimes spot a hawk swimming through the clouds near a sliver of last night's moon or little birds swing-dancing overhead. When I remember to admire the details of God's newborn day, I say a mental prayer of gratitude.

Shortly before 9 a.m., while sitting at my desk in the theology library, I hear a dog barking in the distance. In a few moments, when I glance outside, I see a student in a motorized wheelchair making her way to a nearby classroom building. A paraplegic, she has her black dog tethered to her chair.

Tail wagging, the dog trots carefully beside her, barking a joyous greeting to passers-by. As the two inch their way up the handicapped ramp into the building, I marvel at the woman's determined spirit and the dog's devotion. And I say a prayer for them both.

Afternoon prayer starts when I leave my desk at the library at 11:30 a.m. On afternoons slated for writing, my mind is often crowded with phrases that I'm eager to rush home and record.

At home, I pause to admire the sentinel of our front yard, the squirrel that lives in our birdhouse. When Jef first attached the house to an oak tree, this industrious rodent devoted himself to hours of serious gnawing, eventually widening the doorway sufficiently so he could squeeze inside. Most days, when the animal sees me coming, he pokes his head out and studies me. He doesn't know he's part of my prayer of gratitude.

Afternoon prayer continues when I sit at my desk and—on good days—am blessed with words flowing in an unbroken stream from heart to fingertips. While writing, I sometimes feel like I'm being transported to a shadowy realm outside the borders of reason.

About once a week, I meet my friend, Pam, and her children, Sarah and Stephen, for lunch. Most days, we sit outdoors at nearby, modestly priced cafes and watch the children pretending to be crocodiles or birds. Often, the children tote books from home and request that "Aunt Awaine" (that's me) read aloud to them. As they snuggle up next to me, I thank God for sending these sweet little ones into my life.

Evening prayer starts shortly before bedtime at 9:30, when I check the shape of the night's moon. When she's full and plump, she reminds me of a communion wafer floating in the darkness. When she's just a quarter full, she seems to be grinning at me. I thank God for her loveliness.

In bed, I pray for the people in my life who need help. Sometimes I fall asleep before completing the list, but I don't worry about it.

Verbal requests are lovely, but they're just one way to touch the sacred source of all life. On the days when we pay attention, every moment can be prayer.

6

✴ *Voice of Silence* ✴

Nothing is as vexing as a one-way conversation.

You've probably encountered the well-meaning bore at work who unleashes a torrent of tales about his weekend, his kid, his dog, until your mouth is aching with suppressed yawns. You yearn for the words that never cross his lips: "And what's new with you?"

When it comes to prayer, I must confess I've been a major bore for years.

"God," I beg, "Please take care of…" and then I consult a mental list about two yards long, spanning the spectrum from a friend with a back injury to a dilapidated pooch I once saw ambling down a lonesome road in south Georgia.

My litany of the sick, suffering, and dying completed, I launch into an equally long tirade of personal requests.

"Lord, spare me from melancholy," I implore. "And help me to be a better person."

And so it goes. Finally, my list exhausted, I rise and dust off my knees.

Please don't get me wrong. I'm not suggesting these one-sided conversations don't delight God in some fashion. As a loving father, I surmise He's always pleased to hear from His brood, even if some kids ramble on and on.

But it's unfair to accuse our heavenly Father of not answering our long-winded prayers. After all, we rarely give Him a chance.

"O that today you would listen to His voice," (Psalm 95:7) we are told in the Old Testament. And in the New Testament, Christ reminds us that the sheep always recognize their shepherd's voice and heed only His commands.

But if we're constantly yapping away, how can we hear God's voice?

Troubled by this question, I added a new stitch to my patchwork quilt of prayer a few years ago. I started practicing centering prayer, a Christian practice that resembles the meditative disciplines of Eastern religions.

In his book *Intimacy with God*, Father Thomas Keating explores this Christian practice in which "we consent to God's presence...and gently establish an attitude of waiting upon the Lord with loving attentiveness." When we extract ourselves from our usual flow of thoughts and feelings, Keating writes, our hearts are opened to the divine Spirit and we draw closer to God.

You don't need stained glass, oak pews, or a pulpit. You don't need a Bible, a prayer book, or a candle. You just follow Christ's suggestion: "Whenever you pray, go in to your room and close the door" (Matthew 6:6). Even if you lack a room of your own, you can close the door on the world by shutting your eyes.

You need a quiet place to sit. An overstuffed armchair or a patch of shade beneath a tree will suffice. Then, as the noisy world retreats, you mentally repeat a word like "love" or "peace" to still the ever-rushing tide of thoughts.

Centering prayer is a humbling practice. It won't produce glittering visions of luminescent angels or sparkling revelations. At first, you may feel somewhat antsy and bored. In our frenzied world of faxes, beepers, and cell phones, we rarely find ourselves sitting quietly and doing nothing. Over time, though, some little spaces start appearing between your thoughts. And if you wade gently into the pool of silence that fills your consciousness, you may find something lovely there. Something we too rarely encounter in our lives.

It's the Lord's calling card. It is peace. And it's the voice we've been longing to hear.

7

Small Miracles

Mother's Day used to be a bittersweet holiday. As a childless woman whose mother had died, I'd studiously avoid the shops teeming with cards celebrating the mother-daughter bond. I felt like the proverbial odd duck.

During my twenties I was more concerned with landing a graduate degree than with raising a family. Jef and I married when I was 35, and it was then I started pondering whether motherhood would be in my future. A great waffler, I would mentally list all the reasons we should have a child, and then, in a flash, I'd find myself with a list entitled "on the other hand."

When I confessed my confusion to a friend, she looked amused.

"It's like going swimming," she said. "You don't think about it. You just jump in the pool."

She didn't realize that I waffle even when it comes to swimming. I always wade in, one tiny step at a time.

Well-meaning friends told me all the reasons I should have a child.

"To relive your childhood," said some.

But, unfortunately, my memories of childhood were largely bleak. I remember being sad and anxious a good deal of the time.

"You'll want someone to care for you in your old age," said others.

But it seemed selfish to give birth with the hope of a payback.

"You'd be a wonderful mother," others would insist.

However, when I was around small children for extended periods of time, I found myself getting increasingly frazzled and exhausted. The bottom line was that I didn't feel I had the emotional make-up or necessary energy to handle the endless demands of a small child.

I spent quite a few hours in analysts' offices, mulling over the topic. I read quite a few books. There were days when I felt a real longing for a baby, but then the pendulum would suddenly swing, and I would feel frightened.

After much soul-searching, I reached a conclusion. Since my urge to mother was lukewarm at best—and Jef's urge to father was equally muted—and since a child deserves to be deeply and truly wanted, I decided not to take the plunge.

Since I didn't believe in God at the time, I never considered praying about the decision, nor did I regard a child as a gift freely given by God. Instead, like many women of my generation, I saw the prospect of raising a family as a decision that Jef and I had to make on our own.

Looking back now, however, from the perspective of faith, I feel that God never turned His back on me. Although I wasn't committed to praying, I believe He still was guiding me. I also believe that God "signs off" on the decisions we make sincerely and thoughtfully, and with plenty of soul-searching.

I believe He never called me and Jef to become parents—at least not in the biological sense.

When Jef and I began attending St. Thomas More Church, we also joined the choir. It was there we met Pam, a young woman gifted with an exquisite soprano voice and a very big heart. She and her husband, Chris, both Catholics, had one child—Stephen—and were working on their second. After Mass on Sundays, a group from church would head down to the hall for donuts and coffee. Jef and I became regulars, as did Pam and Chris and Stephen.

Stephen and Jef became good friends, despite their age differences (Stephen was 2 and Jef was 36), because they both loved to draw and shared an interest in hunting unusual and colorful bugs. On Sundays, Stephen would cram his favorite dinosaur toys in his backpack to show his friend.

One day I learned that Pam was facing surgery. Her doctors were concerned about a potentially cancerous growth on one of her ovaries. It was a dicey situation, given that she was two months pregnant at the time, and the doctors didn't advise postponing the surgery until Pam's delivery date. When I heard the news, I started praying daily for her and the baby.

Jef and I prayed the rosary every Sunday afternoon with Mother Teresa's sisters at the Gift of Grace home. When I told the sisters about Pam, one sister gave me a medal to give her. It depicted St. Gerard Majella, the patron saint of pregnant women, and had been blessed by Mother Teresa.

Our prayers were answered. Pam's surgery turned out fine. There was no cancer, and in June of 1998, she gave birth to a healthy girl, named Sarah Evangeline.

And then, after choir practice one night a few months later, Pam asked me a question that would change my life forever.

"Chris and I were wondering if you and Jef might help us out," she said shyly. "We'd like you to be Sarah's godparents."

I still remember the chills of joy that spread all over my body, and the tears that filled my eyes. I realized in that moment that Sarah was to become a great and wonderful gift in our lives.

Standing before the altar on the day of the baptism, holding the plump, bellowing infant in my arms as the priest gently poured water over her head, I felt a deep stirring in my heart. I had an inkling of the love mothers must feel for their children.

Mother's Day was never the same after that. The first year, Pam arrived at the front door, carrying Sarah, who was clutching a tiny box of chocolates, which she eventually relinquished to me, plus a greeting card addressed to "Aunt Lorraine." Every year since then, the twosome has arrived bearing chocolates. This past year, the card had been drawn in crayon by Sarah.

Sarah is now three years old. She and her big brother, Stephen, now 7, call us Uncle Jef and Aunt "Awaine." She makes us feel like family in the tiny, unwitting ways that only a child is capable of, like casually pulling her pacifier from her mouth when she's tired of it, and handing it to us. When we go on walks, the children put their little paws in their Uncle Jef's hand and trot alongside him.

I feel awed by God's generosity in sending us two beautiful children, who may not be "ours" biologically, but who are connected with us on a deep, soulful level.

No one's life is perfect, but I feel we have a choice. We can dwell on the missing faces in our family albums, or we can embrace the larger picture in which we are all parents—and children—in the hearts of others.

8

Heart Whispers

The voice startled me.

I was driving down Ponce de Leon Avenue on my way to the grocery store, when a little voice told me to visit the ornate church on the hill. I'd attended a festival at St. John Chrysostom Melkite Church years ago. I knew the congregation was Eastern Rite Catholic, but that was all I knew.

I struggled against the impulse.

"It's a weekday," I told myself. "No one will be there."

But then I recalled a passage from *The Inner Voice of Love* by Henri J.M. Nouwen.

"You have to trust the inner voice that shows the way," he wrote.

Even though I felt ridiculous, I decided to heed his advice. I pulled off the road and parked in the church lot.

The morning air was stifling and as I climbed from the car, I reflected glumly that this surely had been the worst summer of my life. And not just because of the heat.

I was halfway through seven weeks of daily radiation-therapy treatments for cancer. No matter what I was doing, my grief over my illness would suddenly sneak up behind me, seize me, and drag me down.

To make matters worse, I hadn't written anything in days. Usually my writing flowed effortlessly from a deep secret well inside me. Usually writing was a form of prayer for me. Lately, however, inspiration had been in short supply, and when I checked the word "inspiration" in the dictionary and saw that "guidance by divine influence" was one meaning, I figured I was in serious trouble.

"God has abandoned me," I thought, as I plodded up the steps to the sanctuary.

The door was locked, so I rang the bell at the side door. No answer.

"Give up and go home," my rational mind advised. But another voice, the quieter one, whispered, "Try again."

So I did.

This time the door opened. A stocky, dark-haired man in Bermuda shorts and T-shirt greeted me.

"I'm looking for the priest," I explained.

He smiled widely and gestured toward himself.

"I'm Father John," he said.

"I'd like to make an appointment for confession," I said, surprised by the words that tumbled from my mouth. "I'm going through some hard times."

He nodded and invited me into the sanctuary. While I waited, he disappeared into a side room, where I figured he was consulting his calendar. But, moments later, he appeared at the altar in full priestly garb and gestured for me to stand beside him.

As we stood facing the tabernacle, the priest prayed aloud to the Holy Spirit to guide us. When it was my turn, I blurted out my distress. Sobbing, I told him about feeling abandoned by God. I told him about my illness and my lack of inspiration.

Then Father John said everything I needed to hear. That I was God's beloved daughter. That God would never desert me, even in my darkest hours.

When I knelt down for absolution and he extended an arm gently around my shoulders, I sensed strongly that we were not alone. I felt that someone was listening when he asked God to bless me.

As I was leaving the church, I asked the priest to recommend a good book for me to read. He didn't hesitate.

"Read the gospel of John," he said. "Read it very slowly and listen to what God is saying to you."

I drove home and dug out my Bible. I opened to the gospel of John and read the opening line:

"In the beginning was the Word, and the Word was with God, and the Word was God."

My words had been coming from God all along, I realized. And even if the well had temporarily run dry, I had faith that it would overflow again. I had faith that God was still guiding me.

And now I felt I knew where to find Him. Not in claps of thunder or bolts of lightning. Instead, I'd discover Him in that little voice whispering within my heart.

Questions for Reflection and Discussion

1. How have your daily prayer rituals changed over the years? What did prayer mean to you as a child? What does it mean today?

2. What is it like for you to open your heart to the divine Spirit?

3. What happens when you are "wide awake"?

IV

Suffering

"**I**t's not fair," my friend sobbed over the phone.

Having suffered for years with a serious kidney ailment, she was now losing vision in her left eye.

"I thought I'd paid my dues," she wept.

Another friend fell and injured his back at work. Housebound and in pain for months, he became despondent.

"I'd give this cross to someone else," he sighed, "but who would take it?"

I've asked the question myself hundreds of times. Ever since becoming ill last year, I've wracked my feeble brain trying to make sense of the suffering that seems to be exploding all around me.

But that's the catch. On the surface, it appears random and senseless.

When the disciples encountered a blind man, they asked Christ typical questions that still haunt us today. Why did this happen? Was the man a sinner? Or did his parents sin?

Christ was firm in his reply. No one sinned, He said. But the suffering was not senseless either. The man had been born blind, Christ said, so that "God's works might be revealed in him" (John 9:3).

Christ's explanation mystified me for years. How is God manifested in blindness? I wondered. Or in heart disease? Or in cancer?

Of course, there is no one-size-fits-all answer to the dilemma of human suffering. But making a radical shift in my perspective helped me glimpse some elements of grace in my own predicament.

I had to stop peering into the mirror and obsessing over my own reflection. Instead, when I started focusing on the people around me, what I saw was surprising. I saw a throng of people who couldn't take away my cross, but who were nonetheless bending under its weight.

One of my cross bearers was a man whose name I never learned. I met him in the basement of a nearby hospital in the radiation department. On the day of my surgery, his job was to monitor a gigantic machine that took multiple images of a dye that had been injected into my breast. My job was to lie perfectly still.

We talked. All I know about him is that he lives alone and has a dog. But his kindness touched me in a way I'll never forget. When the films were completed, he arranged a blanket in a wheelchair for me with as much care as if he were preparing a crib for the baby Jesus. Once I settled in, he gently arranged the blanket around my legs.

I may never see this man again, but I'll never forget him. And I believe that whenever we are stricken by disease, heartbreak, or injury, people like him surround us.

But we have to notice them.

We have to turn our gaze momentarily from the cross and look instead at the crowd, praying and weeping, gathered beneath. We have to turn our eyes from the person in the mirror—or in the hospital bed—to the friends and relatives standing nearby.

We may still rage against the suffering. And we may still protest the unfairness of our burdens. But if we glimpse the little bud of compassion that miraculously blossoms in the desert of pain, we may discover meaning in our suffering. And we may even see God's works revealed there.

9

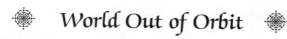 *World Out of Orbit*

Sometimes we get jaded by the humdrum trickle of everyday life.

Oh, yes, there's the blaze of sunrise. The robin that shows up daily for a dunk in the birdbath. And the moon swelling proudly in the night sky.

But it all seems so terribly predictable. So uneventful. Until something happens that knocks our whole world out of orbit.

For me it was a call from the hospital. It seems my recent mammogram wasn't quite up to snuff. Seems I had to return for another round of X-rays.

Dashing to the hospital on I-285 in a wild sea of cars, I was dismayed to realize on a deep soulful level what I'd acknowledged only superficially before. It's a big world out there and it will go on spinning just fine without me.

As I paced in the waiting room, my mind treated me to an instant replay of my life's major events. While the other women sat placidly reading magazines, I asked myself the big question.

"Do I have any regrets?" I wondered.

Unfortunately, Katherine Hepburn has spoiled that question for me forever.

"Of course I do," she sniffed in an interview years ago. "Only an idiot doesn't have regrets."

Well, maybe I'm an idiot, but I don't have any. At least no big ones. I've never been to Europe, but that's fine with me. I'm not much of a traveler. And I never pined to be rich or tall, so there are no problems there either.

When I was a kid, my longings were fairly low-key. I yearned to turn out a decent lasagna, learn to drive, marry a nice man, and grow roses. My lasagna could use some help—but I can be happy with three out of four.

After the X-rays, I was ushered into a small lonely room, where, moments later, a somber radiologist delivered the news. I'd need a biopsy on my breast to determine whether or not I had cancer.

Driving home, I kept switching on the windshield wipers, even though the sky was clear. It was tears, I finally realized. Still, I didn't feel inclined to shake my fist at heaven and yell, "Why me, God?" After all, I never asked "Why me?" when He gave me loving parents, a good marriage, a nice home.

And as the cars streamed by, I realized I wasn't alone. Many of the faces I glimpsed behind the glass shields looked worn and worried. Maybe they were praying for a sick child, a dying uncle, a despondent friend. Maybe they were also driving home from the hospital with shattering news.

It was agonizing waiting to see the surgeon about the biopsy. But my friends and family rallied in the most loving way. One friend, confined to bed rest during her pregnancy, sent me encouraging scriptural passages in the mail. My mother-in-law called often to "check on her little bird."

And my best friend showed up at the front door with the surest antidote to the blues ever invented—my little goddaughter, Sarah, who danced on my bed while singing a rousing rendition of "Jingle Bells," and then gave me a generous smooch on the cheek.

The surprising outpouring of gifts continued. My internist gave me the biggest bear hug of my life. My pastor promised to anoint me with holy oil the day before the operation.

But, hands-down, the award for love and compassion went to my husband, whose shoulder was getting a little soggy. He said the words every woman longs to hear: "No matter what happens, we'll face it together."

And I know we will. In the meantime, I'm sitting by the front window to see the fire in the morning sky, to glimpse the punctual robin wallowing in the bath in mid-afternoon, and to return the moon's goodnight smile.

How ordinary it all is. And how infinitely precious.

10

✸ Change of Heart ✸

I noticed the woman the moment I walked into the lobby. Shaking and sobbing uncontrollably, she was talking to someone on the phone. I couldn't hear what she was saying, yet I felt a strong urge to comfort her. But something stopped me. She's a stranger, I reminded myself, and it's none of your business. I didn't want to be late for my appointment, so I hurried down the hall.

My yearly mammogram had shown "suspicious" areas. I was here this morning to talk with the surgeon who would perform a biopsy on my breast.

After the operation was scheduled, my friends and family members told me I was in their prayers. Some friends encouraged me with scriptural verses.

"Ask and you will receive," one enthused. "If you pray in Jesus' name," another assured me, "you will receive healing."

And so I prayed. While gardening, while showering, while driving. I did more than that—I shamelessly begged God for a good outcome. By the day of the biopsy, I was so wracked with worry I'd lost five pounds. After the procedure, I went home to collapse on my bed and storm heaven some more.

Two days later, the surgeon called to deliver the news that would change my life forever. The biopsy had shown the presence of cancer. As I wept over the phone, he assured me that in six months, I would look back and be glad I'd had the mammogram. But all I could remember was my mother's face as she lay dying of breast cancer. And I cried again.

As I told the dreadful news to all the people who'd been praying for me, I began to feel that perhaps I'd done something terribly wrong. Maybe I'd missed some vital part of the prayer formula. Maybe I didn't have the proper relationship with God. Worst of all, maybe He didn't love me enough to answer my pleas for healing.

These were agonizing thoughts. I began a mental journey into my past to probe my relationship with God. As a child, I'd been spoon fed an image of God as an old man in the sky with a long, white beard. The nuns had told me God was my heavenly father, but that was little help for me. My earthly father was emotionally distant, a man so puzzled by the whole parenting endeavor that he rarely showed his daughters any affection. I hoped my heavenly father wasn't as standoffish.

Later I discovered that many religions defined God as love. Since God had no limits, I figured that His love would be boundless too. It would be a pure, unconditional love, I decided. This made sense to me, although it was hard to imagine how it would feel to be so loved. In my childhood, love had been doled out with strings attached. If I got gold stars on my spelling tests, my mom toasted my success. If I brought home a "B," she seemed disappointed.

When I learned about Jesus, I was truly comforted. Here was a man of fiery, swelling emotions, a man who passionately celebrated life. He loved His friends, embraced children, cherished the suffering masses. He gave us a new commandment and it was all about love.

But Christ suffered the most horrible death imaginable. And He had the added burden of knowing the exact details ahead of time. That He'd be slowly tortured and nailed to a cross. That He'd suffocate in the broiling sun. That there'd be no relief for His pain.

No wonder He sweated blood the night before his death. No wonder He pleaded with His father to "take the cup from me." Still, He realized that prayers are requests, not demands, and so He added: "Not my will, but thy will be done."

Like Christ, I've done my share of begging.

"Please, dear God," I've whimpered, "don't let this be cancer."

But now the cup has been passed to me and I've reluctantly taken a sip. The taste is bitter, just as I feared. But I keep reminding myself that Christ tapped into new life after His agony, and perhaps I will experience some sort of enlightenment myself.

Maybe, in some small ways, it's already happening. Until recently, I've been pretty skilled at avoiding the suffering masses. Oh, I did my share of volunteer work, but it was all tidy and neat. When it came down to brushing shoulders with the decrepit and dying, I fled. I considered doing volunteer work at a local hospital, but I feared getting too involved emotionally.

Ironically enough, I'm now spending much of my time at that hospital. Since my diagnosis, the medical center has become a second home. And lately it's becoming more difficult for me to block out the faces of the worried, broken people who stream endlessly through the doors. People facing surgery, chemotherapy, radiation therapy. People trembling in fear. People just like me.

I still whine and complain about my illness. I still grieve for the days when I didn't have to struggle daily with the blues. But every so often, I notice some small secret door opening in my heart. It's a door that was sealed before.

And perhaps this is God's answer to my prayers. A heart that mysteriously is starting to awaken. A heart that may stretch larger over time.

Sometimes I envision the woman I saw that morning in the lobby. The woman who was sobbing into the phone. The next time I see someone in such distress, I won't miss my chance. I'll know just what to do. I'll brush aside my fears about impropriety and give her a big hug.

I don't think it will be difficult to do. After all, that woman was me.

11

❖ Jack-in-the-Box God ❖

I had a jack-in-the-box when I was a kid. It played a perky tune and then—WHAM!—out popped a hideous puppet with an evil grin. I always expected Jack to shout, "Gotcha!"

Evidently some people see God that way.

The Rev. Jerry Falwell and broadcaster Pat Robertson, commenting on the September 11, 2001, terrorist attacks, claimed the United States had insulted God and "lost divine protection."

"God . . . allowed the enemies of America to give us probably what we deserve," Falwell noted.

The belief in a vengeful jack-in-the-box God is all too common. A fervent churchgoer, my aunt once said, "My job is going well. My marriage is back on track." And then a furtive look crossed her face. "I'd better not jinx it."

Perhaps she feared God would burst into her life unexpectedly, saying, "You think everything is fine? Well, gotcha!"

In the movie *Night of the Iguana,* a pastor tells his congregation he refuses to conduct services in praise of the "angry, petulant old man" whom it worships.

"You have turned your backs on the God of love and compassion," he roars, "and invented for yourselves a cruel, senile delinquent."

If people like Jerry Falwell and Pat Robertson want to worship a cruel and mean-spirited God, that's their prerogative. But I wish they wouldn't call themselves "Christians."

Christ was light years removed from being a vengeful, blood-thirsty person. He described Himself as "gentle and humble of heart." He invited the weary to come to Him for rest.

"I came that they may have life, and have it abundantly" (John 10:10), He told us.

The gospels overflow with scenes of Him embracing life. You see Him filling wine glasses at a wedding feast, dining with friends, welcoming children.

Abundant life sounds terrific, you might reply, but what about fractured legs, broken hearts, and dashed dreams? What about thousands suffering and dying in the terrorist attacks? What about the grieving children left behind?

Unfortunately, there is no neat and tidy answer. At the heart of Christianity is a wrenching paradox. God's beloved son suffered a hideous death, but this death gave us something immeasurably precious: a glimpse of the divine heart.

Christ sampled the whole spectrum of human life. He wept at His friend's death, took pity on the hungry, and anguished in the Garden of Gethsemane. In His breast beat a human heart, capable of intense love—and suffering.

Perhaps the image of a suffering God would cause the Rev. Jerry Falwell and Pat Robertson to blow a gasket. But their jack-in-the-box version is a cruel travesty.

It's infuriating to implicate God in terrorism. Human beings are capable of stunning acts of goodness—as witnessed in the lives of Mahatma Gandhi, Mother Teresa, and the New York firefighters—and horrendous evil deeds, as evidenced by the hijackings.

The lesson of the terrorist attacks is not that God was punishing us. The lesson is that when His children are in pain, He suffers too.

God was weeping on the morning of September 11. He was weeping in the hearts of the passengers en route to their violent destinations. And in the hearts of the people lost in the carnage of the Pentagon and World Trade Center.

And when we feel crushed by grief over these terrible acts of man's inhumanity to man—and to God—our creator doesn't gloat. He doesn't jump out and shout: "Gotcha!"

Instead, He stretches out a hand. It's a hand that is bruised and pierced. But it will lift us up, again and again.

Questions for Reflection and Discussion

1. Have you ever experienced, or accompanied a loved one through a serious illness that knocked your world out of orbit?

2. How did God make His presence known to you in your suffering?

3. What is your reaction to the image of a jack-in-the-box God? What about a suffering God?

V

Forgiving

I still recall how frightened I felt, standing in the confessional line when I was a little kid. "Bump, thump, whump," went my heart, and "churn, gurgle, burn," went my stomach.

It wasn't that I had grave sins to confess. After all, there's not much damage a 7-year old girl can do in a week, and I was vigilant in showing up every Saturday at the little confessional booth.

Instead, I was fretting about getting the details just right.

I knew I was supposed to say, "Bless me, Father, for I have sinned" at the beginning, and "For these and all the sins of my life, I am sorry" at the end. I also knew I had to carefully enumerate my laundry list of sins and then say the Act of Contrition, a somewhat long-winded prayer peppered with mysterious words like "heartily," "detest," "offend," and "resolve."

In my teenage years, as my sins took on more vigor and luster, I feared I might one day let slip a sin that would create an uproar in the confessional. I pictured the priest swinging wide his door and rushing to my side of the confessional.

"Young lady, we're going to see your parents about *this* sin," he'd roar.

Of course, I knew about the priestly vow of confidentiality, but when you're a teen, you don't trust adults to hold up their end of the bargain. Anything was possible in a world where grown-ups often said, "I promise"—and then later forgot.

I especially dreaded having to say aloud that I'd had "impure thoughts" again that week, even though I'd admitted to the same mischief the previous Saturday. Worse yet, I didn't want the young and handsome priest who taught high school religion to suspect that he himself often had a starring role in my naughty day-dreams.

I didn't understand why I couldn't banish indelicate thoughts once and for all. If I were truly good, if I were in the least bit like the saints I'd read about at school, why was I standing in the con-fessional line, week after week, with the same list of wrongdoings? Disobeying, lying, arguing, fantasizing. The standard flaws of my youth were utterly predictable.

Today, so many years later, I still cringe at telling another human being about my shortcomings, but my reticence is over-shadowed by the intense relief I experience when I walk out the door.

No doubt about it, my sins lack the luster they once had in my youth. The list has changed drastically. Arguing with my sister is a thing of the past. We now chat amiably on the phone. I have no parents to disobey. And scandalous thoughts are few and far between.

A few years ago, I was morosely unveiling my laundry list of sins to a priest in a rather niggling fashion, as in the days of my youth. "I missed Mass twice. I lied three times," etc.

Interrupting me, he suddenly took my hand and smiled. "Christ came to bring us joy," he said. And I had to laugh.

I'm afraid I so often miss the "joy" thing. A rather melancholy soul, I often forget that the crucifixion was one chapter in the life of a man who lived joyfully for 33 years. He came to give us abundant life. He came to teach us about love. And He said, over and over, "Peace be with you."

Perhaps our failure to really live as fully as Christ did could be a sin that many of us fail to confess. And I wonder what the penance would be.

I imagine the priest leaning forward and saying, "Spend a day in a field of wildflowers. Sit on the bank of the creek and watch the chipmunks scooting up and down the rocks. Go fishing. Dance at a wedding. And, for God's sake, get rid of the laundry list."

12

His Trespasses

When I asked my friend's little daughter what her dad enjoyed doing in his spare time, she didn't miss a beat.

"Anything to do with me," she beamed.

I rejoiced for her, of course, but I also felt a stinging regret. My dad's free time rarely included his two daughters. And although he's been dead over twenty years, I still puzzle over those early days.

Oh, there were moments. Once he took us to a farm and pointed out the curl on a baby pig's tail. Another time he treated us to hamburgers at an amusement park near our home.

It's not that our family was fractured by a troubled marriage. Soul-mates, my mom and dad had a relationship that lasted 35 years with hardly a snag. The family photos show them—the dark-eyed Tom and his beloved Grace—cheek to cheek over a birthday cake or embracing at the ocean's edge. He continued to woo her even after they had married, showing up on Valentine's Day with chocolates encased in a furry red heart and on Easter with a pot of satiny white lilies.

But he seemed mystified by the whole fatherhood thing. Back home after a shopping spree with our mom, my sister and I would model our purchases for our dad, twirling around and praying silently for compliments. Gazing curiously at the starchy dresses and pointy-toed shoes, he'd inquire: "Are they comfortable?" Sighing, we assured him they were.

He wasn't one to dole out hugs and kisses to his girls, so when I craved attention, I ran to my mom, trailing her adoringly around the house as she vacuumed.

"You're the most beautiful woman in the world," I intoned often—and I meant it.

I agonized over the prim families on "Father Knows Best" and "Leave It to Beaver." Were there really dads who wore snappy suits and sagely divulged life's meaning to their kids? Were there really dads who called their daughters "princess"? And daughters who cast adoring glances at their dads?

Kids can be horrible snobs about their fathers and I was no exception. Sometimes I was ashamed because he had only a sixth-grade education. His passions were smoking Cuban cigars, betting at the horse races, and playing poker.

Try as I might, I couldn't picture Ward Cleaver poring over the racing results in the newspaper or counting his chips at a card game. Nor could I imagine him blowing a fuse at the supper table after a kid knocked over a glass of milk or, belt in hand, chasing the kids around the house.

Not that our dad ever hit us. The belt was merely a scare tactic—and it worked famously. But it must have pained him to see me and my sister cowering behind our mom because later he'd show up with comic books as peace offerings.

Away at college, I'd phone home every weekend. If he answered, I groped for words while imagining what a cinch it'd be for the "Father Knows Best" gal.

"This is Princess," she'd purr.

I took the easy way out: "Is mom there?" I inquired.

When I was 25, the unthinkable happened. My mom was stricken with cancer. She had always been the letter writer in the family, punctuating her notes to me with little hearts and tiny x's for kisses. After her death, my dad began writing letters to me on big yellow legal pads, sometimes surprising me with his dry wit. In one letter, he inquired about the health of my overweight cat and admonished me not to spend the enclosed check entirely on cat treats.

In another letter, he proposed we take a cruise together to the Bahamas. I was intrigued by the invitation since we'd never had a father-daughter outing before. On the first day of my spring break, I drove to his condo in Ft. Lauderdale and the next day we gathered up our suitcases and headed to the ship.

Neither of us could have predicted that my mother's absence would be almost palpable in such surroundings. No matter where my father and I went, it seemed we'd forgotten something. I kept imagining how she would have loved the vast ocean churning around us and the snazzy turquoise sky. I kept imagining that I saw her out of the corner of my eye.

One evening I found my father hunched over on a chaise lounge on the ship's deck. He was weeping. He missed her. And as I sat beside him, speechless, I forgave him everything in that moment. I realized that all along he and I had shared a great treasure. Our souls had found their moorings in the same person—his wife, my mother.

Maybe he wore Bermuda shorts instead of Brooks Brothers. Maybe he never taught me how to light a campfire. And maybe he never figured out how to navigate through the dizzying waters of fatherhood. But he did give me something immeasurably precious.

He taught me about a fierce love that endures forever. And somehow, that makes up for it all.

13

The Least of These

I spotted the baby in the gardening section of the store. While his parents were scrutinizing tomato plants, the baby perched in his stroller, watching intently. He had a head of lazy blonde curls, stout legs, and a round face.

"What a beautiful boy!" I exclaimed, and both parents smiled proudly. "He could pose for a baby food ad, he's so healthy looking," I added.

At that moment, the tiny stranger beamed me a toothless smile and stretched his plump hands toward me. Gently I grasped the little paws in a delicate handshake.

The encounter was a small, seemingly insignificant, event. Yet, in the old days, I would have reacted in a remarkably different way. I certainly wouldn't have stopped to talk to the baby. Instead, I would have walked quickly away, overcome with grief.

A terrible, raw guilt had festered in me for many years. Ever since the day I'd walked into a trendy women's clinic and filled out the paperwork for what I believed was a simple medical procedure. At the time I was an ardent feminist as well as an atheist. I had studied ethics in graduate school and was fully versed in all the philosophical arguments for and against this particular procedure. I firmly believed that abortion was morally acceptable if performed in the early stages of a pregnancy. I firmly believed that a woman's rights took precedence over the rights of the fetus.

None of the philosophical articles ever suggested that the "procedure" might be any more life changing than, say, a tooth extraction. Instead, the authors had led me to believe that some "tissue" would be removed. That would be the end of the story—or so I thought. The articles also failed to mention that I might experience searing pain, so intense that I nearly ripped the hand off the woman who stood by my side, her eyes shining with compassion.

Even though I didn't believe that what I had done was morally wrong, some instinct told me not to tell people afterwards. Instead, I lived under a crushing weight of secrecy. As the years wore on, I found it puzzling that I never encountered a woman who spoke openly of having an abortion. There seemed to be an invisible veil of shame covering the issue, even among women who apparently saw no moral problems with it.

Gradually I discovered that my emotions pulsed to a very different beat than my intellect. Every time I saw an infant, my immediate reactions were always the same.

"How old would my child be now?" I'd agonize. "What would my child have looked like?"

These questions hounded me for years. Still, when I returned to Catholicism many years after the incident, I clung tightly to my intellectual stance on abortion. Despite my own emotional turmoil over my experience, I still believed that a woman should have dominion over her body. Then one day in the library, I happened upon a book about Mother Teresa. It didn't take many pages to convince me that she was an extraordinarily holy woman, but I was perplexed by her vehement rejection of abortion. She's a virtuous woman, I told myself, but very old-fashioned and seriously out of touch with the realities faced by contemporary women like myself.

A few days later, the priest read one of Mother Teresa's favorite scriptural passages at Mass: "Just as you did it to one of the least of these, you did it to me" (Matthew 25:39).

A claw of grief clutched my heart. With great effort I managed to stem the tide of tears rising within me. In an agonizing moment of guilt, I finally realized why Mother Teresa was so protective of the unborn, the elderly, and the dying. She knew whom Christ was referring to when He'd mentioned the "least of these."

I began having flashbacks in which I re-lived the experience over and over. Each time, I saw myself walking into the clinic and climbing up on the table. I felt the crushing pain. I saw the woman standing beside me holding my hand. Wracked with guilt and self-loathing, I wept. How could I have ended my child's life?

One day, I summoned up my courage and turned to a priest in the confessional, sobbing as I blurted out the story. He listened quietly and then gently reminded me of Jesus' words on the cross, "Father, forgive them, for they do not know what they are doing" (Luke 23:34). As the storm of tears continued, the priest explained that I hadn't realized at the time that I was taking a life. Just as Jesus had forgiven the people who'd nailed Him to the cross, He would forgive me too. But one question gnawed at me still.

"Father," I stammered, "what happened to that little soul?"

The priest paused only a moment before replying in a gentle voice: "God takes care of the little souls."

A great burden was lifted. God had forgiven me, I realized, as I left the confessional.

In the weeks to come, I repeated the priest's words mentally over and over: "God takes care of the little souls." But the feeling of relief was short-lived and just a few months later, the flashbacks returned. Maybe God had forgiven me, but I hadn't forgiven myself.

One day, I saw a small notice in our church bulletin about a Catholic group called "PATH: Post-Abortion Treatment and Healing." The words seemed to jump off the page at me. When I dialed the phone number, the woman who answered had the kindest voice I'd ever heard. Her name was Mary Anne.

When we met, she listened to every detail of my story. Then she assured me that many other women share the same emotional responses of regret and self-recrimination that I was experiencing. She explained that grieving must come before healing, and since I'd never really grieved, I'd never had the chance to heal.

In our meetings over the next few months, Mary Anne allowed me time to grieve. She gave me a workbook written for Christian women who'd had an abortion. The book contained a series of questions, plus Biblical passages for reflection and discussion. I wept as I reflected and I wept as I discussed my answers with Mary Anne. But there was one question I couldn't answer: "Where was God during the procedure?" When I told Mary Anne that I'd left that one blank, she looked puzzled but said nothing.

Gradually, I noticed a subtle shift in my emotional landscape. By the time we'd finished reading the book, I'd made the journey through a dark tunnel of grief and had emerged at a place where I could finally start to forgive myself.

That was four years ago. Just the other day, I unearthed the book and read the scrawled responses that I'd written. I pondered anew the one question I hadn't been able to answer. It still puzzled me.

I finally found the answer one night when I awoke from a deep sleep. I realized why I'd left the space blank. It was because of my firm conviction that God couldn't possibly have been there in the clinic with me. The blank space revealed my belief that, just as I'd given up on God, He had given up on me.

But then I remembered Mother Teresa's favorite passage again. And I remembered her conviction that God disguises Himself, appearing in our lives in unexpected ways. In the hungry and the thirsty. In prisoners, in children—and in strangers.

At that moment, I finally realized why Mary Anne had seemed mystified when I'd told her about the blank space in the book. I think she'd suspected where God had been that day.

Even if I hadn't recognized Him, God had been right there in the clinic with me. But He had been concealed within the heart of someone else. And even though I had deserted Him, He had never abandoned me. He was right there in the heart of that woman who had stood faithfully by my side, holding my hand.

14

⁕ Daddy God ⁕

"Just wait until your father gets home."

My mom's famous warning often chilled my heart when I was a child. When my weary dad arrived home, she'd give him the low-down on the kids' transgressions—and then he'd remove his belt and chase my sister and me around the house.

Although I don't remember my dad ever hitting us, the ritual served its purpose. We learned to fear him.

In catechism classes the nuns said God was my heavenly father. Not surprisingly, I drew a mental picture of God as a big, frightening daddy in the sky.

This daddy in the sky kept a running tally of my misdeeds. He knew when I dipped my hand in the cookie jar. He knew when I taunted my sister. And if I didn't amend my ways, He'd one day hurl me into an eternal pit of fire. When my teachers assured me that "God loves you," I was skeptical.

As I grew up, my relationship with God was starched and formal. I mouthed the prescribed prayers and followed the hallowed rituals. If I misbehaved, I expected a giant fist of doom to strike me down. When nothing happened, I figured God was just biding His time. Maybe it wasn't very surprising when I declared myself an atheist in college. I'd had enough of the forbidding image of a Daddy God.

When I finally returned to the Church, I realized that the spiritual landscape of my childhood needed revamping. My image of the Daddy God clashed furiously with the tender figure of His son, who had described Himself as "gentle and humble."

As I began the arduous task of dethroning the Daddy God, I was fortunate to discover a kindred spirit. Her name is Julian of Norwich, a 14th century mystic whose visions brought her face to face with Christ. In her book, *Revelations of Divine Love,* Julian recorded her encounters with a deity who lacked even a shred of anger and vengeance. Instead, she beheld a God of endless affection and mercy.

"I saw that He is everything good and comforting and helpful," she wrote. He envelops us in love, she added, "embracing us and guiding us in all things."

Still, the old figures from my childhood sometimes assert themselves. First and foremost is an angry Mother Superior in a crow-black habit.

"It's fear of God—not love—that keeps people from sinning," she protests.

But I believe love is a stronger motivator than fear. And I believe we will not deceive, abuse, neglect, rob or kill our neighbors if we deeply—and truly—love them and love God.

Surely the taste of sin grows bitter as we tap into the nectar of divine affection. That's why Christ, who radiated kindness, assured us that, "Whoever loves me will keep my word" (John 14:15).

Some nights that old Daddy God still haunts me. He thunders over the terrain of my dreams, brandishing a list of my wrongdoings. He threatens to extract a fearful revenge.

Still, I remain hopeful, praying that someday the script will change. And sometimes I imagine Him calling my name. I see myself creeping from the shadows and turning to face Him at last. And then I picture the old Daddy God doing something totally out of character. Something I rarely remember my earthly father ever doing.

He throws away the list. Then He leans down—and He embraces me.

Questions for Reflection and Discussion

1. Give examples of times in your life when you have experienced God's compassion and forgiveness.

2. How can we forgive ourselves, once God has forgiven us?

3. How do the gospel scenes that reveal Christ's mercy affect you?

VI

Simplifying

I still remember the day when I learned that my friend's new-born baby, Peter, had been rushed to intensive care. He was having heart trouble.

"What can I do?" I asked.

The answer was straightforward enough. His mother, Josephine, needed companionship as she camped out day and night at the hospital. Without hesitation, I rushed to her side.

At one time, that simple gesture would have been impossible. I was working at a high-stress job far from home. The job, including the commute, drained my life of over ten hours a day. I had little energy—and hardly any time—to extend myself to others.

My daily life seemed sadly disconnected from my faith. I was haunted by the biblical passage where the Lord tells Peter that we show our love for God by feeding His sheep. How, I fretted, can we feed His sheep if we spend our days in traffic snarls, client meetings, and power lunches?

It seemed an impossible dilemma—until I changed my attitude toward money.

When Jef and I got married in 1982, we were big-time spenders. A stream of cash flowed into our lives at payday and promptly dwindled away. Savings? We'd work on that tomorrow.

Then, in 1993 a friend gave us *Your Money or Your Life* by Joe Dominguez and Vicki Robin, a provocative book that promised to transform the reader's relationship with money. The authors presented nine steps that had allowed Dominguez to leave paid employment when he was 30. He'd devoted the rest of his life to community service.

The book revealed an antidote to the frenzied pace of our lives, but it demanded some serious soul-searching. Before snaring a shiny new gizmo, we had to learn to ask ourselves: "Will this object bring me true fulfillment? Does it click with my values?" and "How would we spend our days if the doctors told us we had only a year left?"

Me-centered activities like cruising the mall seemed a pitiful answer.

Gradually, we stopped squandering money and dug our way out of debt. We checked out books from the library, packed lunches from home, and bought clothes in thrift stores. Most importantly, we asked ourselves, over and over, a telling question: "Do we have enough?"

Did we have enough clothing, furniture, jewelry, and gadgets? Overwhelmingly, our answer was "yes." It didn't make sense to keep amassing more and more stuff.

A few years after reading the book, we made some big changes. We sold our vacation home in Florida and before long, we were merrily burning the mortgage papers on our Georgia home in the fireplace. We were finally debt-free.

But something was still missing. It was that precious commodity called time.

I wanted to get involved in my church and community, but I was puzzled. How could I respond to the desperate plea of a friend while I was working full time? Emergencies don't always happen on weekends.

One day, while sitting at my desk, I had a vision of my epitaph. I feared it would read: "She made a good salary with nice benefits—and she dreamed of someday helping others."

In 1999, I took a big leap of faith. I climbed down the career ladder, bid farewell to my lucrative job with all the trimmings, and became a free-lance writer. Much to my surprise, I am now much wealthier than I was before, although my riches are reflected not in bills and coins but in hours, minutes, and seconds.

Now there's time to take my 86-year-old friend to lunch and play with Sarah, my tiny goddaughter, and her brother, Stephen. Time to visit the nursing home and join a discussion group at church. One day I spent five hours cuddling baby Peter at the hospital while his mom took a break. In the old days, I would have been too busy.

Of course, simplifying has its sacrifices. You can't sweep through the mall triumphantly brandishing charge cards. You can't dress in the trendiest clothes or zip through town in the sleekest car.

Still, there are lovely benefits.

Last Sunday, I became the proud godmother of baby Peter, whose health is on the upswing. He was all spruced up in a dapper outfit and his cheeks were rosy.

But when his parents and grandma thanked me profusely for helping them, I felt a little uncomfortable.

I felt that somehow I should be the one thanking them. After all, they gave me a lovely chance to feed the Lord's sheep.

15

 Ospreys, Hermits, and Vacation Homes

One day on vacation in Florida, Jef and I spotted a hermit crab trying on a new shell.

This house-hunting task is a predictable part of a hermit crab's life, for with every increase in girth, the animal's abode grows snugger and the need for a roomier dwelling place becomes a high priority.

As we watched, the crab poked out his head and claws to examine the potential new piece of real estate. I imagined him ticking off the requirements: solid construction, decent weight, good drainage. Evidently the shell passed the test, for the animal quickly abandoned his old home, slipped into the new one, and trundled down the shore.

Like the hermit crab, Jef and I were content with temporary housing when we first visited the island of Cedar Key in 1988. We were fortunate to find a small condo to rent that had everything we required for a sparkling time—a lovely kitchen, comfy porch, and easy access to the sea.

Visit after visit, we returned to the same condo, getting a kick out of reading other visitors' comments in the guest book and adding our own. "Saw roseate spoonbills today." "Watched sea otters in the marshes." And so it went.

As the years passed, we started itching to own a piece of the island. One night, we casually stopped by a realtor's office to check out land prices. Before long, we were driving around looking at—and lusting over—island properties.

When we discovered a plot of land in the marshes with an affordable price tag, we jumped. It had live oaks and palmetto trees where we could tie up our boat, the Sea Moose, between visits. It had its own dock. We told ourselves that someday we might build a home there.

Someday came sooner than we expected. As our visits to the island became more frequent, our yearning for a place of our own skyrocketed. Before long, we decided to take the plunge and build a home in the marshes, which would be a vacation home until we eventually moved to Cedar Key full time.

The stilt house was completed in January of 1991. And it was beautiful—small but lovely. Sporting cedar planks on the outside and knotty-pine wood floors inside, it hovered handsomely over the marshes like an egret.

We were thrilled that we could sit outside on our very own dock—and if the mosquitoes weren't out in droves—watch blue crabs moseying about just beneath the water's surface. We could throw in a crab trap filled with smelly mullet heads and pull in supper a few hours later.

On nights as black as India ink, we could stand on our front porch and—if the mosquitoes weren't out in droves—listen to the hopeful calls of the whippoorwills.

The mosquitoes weren't the only sour notes in our newfound paradise. There were also "no-see-ums," tiny, almost invisible flies with voracious appetites and the supernatural ability to slip through screens. Under a microscope, I suspect the "no-see-um" would proudly reveal itself as 1 part body, 99 parts mouth. At low tide, these little guys emerged from some secret place in the mud to clamp their jaws on our flesh.

Still, there was an abundance of beauty everywhere. Pelicans and ibis flew by our porch every day. Black-crowned night herons and snowy egrets fished lazily in the canal and hunted snakes in the tall grasses nearby. An osprey a few houses away provided us with plenty of laughs as she busied herself constructing a nest atop a neighbor's TV antenna.

Despite such magical moments, it wasn't long before the bright edge on our once-carefree vacations started dulling as the problems associated with owning a second home began surfacing. Before, our vacations had merely required packing our bags and heading to the rented condo. Owning a vacation home, however, spawned a seemingly endless to-do list. We were faced with costly repairs and upkeep—mowing the yard, trimming the trees, touching up paint, and patching the roof.

And then there were the critters.

The home was routinely invaded either by marching battalions of ants, small birds who enjoyed nesting in the attic, or turtle-sized Palmetto bugs who scampered gaily through the kitchen. On each visit, we'd survey the damages and then get to work patching and cleaning.

One day, Jef and I faced reality. The island lacked two essentials for us to lead a happy, fulfilled life—a Catholic church (the nearest one was thirty miles away) and decent job prospects. There was little chance we would ever move permanently to our beloved island.

Once this realization hit, we began questioning the American dream that celebrates owning a second home with as much reverence as the discovery of the Holy Grail.

The hermit crab selects a home out of necessity, not because he fancies a second shell. And what about us? We couldn't really say we had needed the vacation home. Instead, we realized we'd fallen prey to the widespread belief that "more is better."

One evening on a walk, Jef and I noticed an osprey's nest perched upon a telephone pole. Ospreys are renowned for their roomy and dramatic nests, imaginatively crafted from whatever materials the birds can scavenge from people's yards and garbage dumps. This nest was particularly flamboyant, sporting many types of rope and twine intermingled with twigs, bits of old fishing nets, and gaudy strips of cast-off clothing.

The tiny birds living at the bottom of this gigantic structure evidently were hitching a ride on the ground floor of the osprey's residence, thereby gaining all the security afforded by the big bird's hard work—without having to lift a wing.

The little birds hadn't spent hours planning the layout of the nest or searching for the right materials. After a storm, they wouldn't be bothered repairing the structure. They could simply go elsewhere.

They were renters. They were living relatively worry free. And they were smart.

In the old days, we'd had everything we needed to have a smashing good time on our trips. A little condo where someone else had mended the screens, trimmed the trees, and paid the utilities, taxes, and insurance. Our job had been to enjoy ourselves.

The prospect of selling the marsh house tugged at my heart. I feared that releasing our grip on the house meant abandoning our precious island. It took some serious reflection to realize that having a house on the island didn't entitle us to possess the marshes, the birds, or the stunning sunsets. They were all free.

After we sold the house in 1997, we became renters again. We returned to the same small condo we had once enjoyed years before—and found it delightful.

On vacations these days, we still love watching the sun emerge flamboyantly each morning. We still mosey over to the airport to witness the ibis' migration at sunset. And we still occasionally try our hands at crabbing and fishing.

The hermit crabs and the birds seem to know a secret about ownership that we humans struggle with all our lives. We don't have to own things to enjoy them. Marjorie Kinnan Rawlings' words in *Cross Creek* beautifully tell the tale: "We are tenants, and not possessors" of the land, she noted. "The earth may be borrowed, but not bought. It may be used, but not owned."

And so with islands too. In the end, Cedar Key belongs to the otters, the mullet, the whippoorwill, to the birds hitching a ride on the osprey's nest—and to the hermit crabs, living quite joyfully in their temporary little homes.

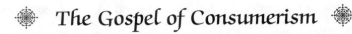 The Gospel of Consumerism

Unhappiness is good for business. Take it from someone who knows.

Since childhood, I've lamented over my looks. Condemning my hair as too straight or too fine, too frizzy or too dull, I've spent a small fortune on hairspray, conditioners, and mousse.

My skin also has been a constant torment. When I was a teenager, I blew my allowance on medicated lotions and gels. These days the new demon is wrinkles.

Recently, a saleslady slathered my cheeks with a cream she swore would banish "fine lines." Falling for her pitch, I scurried home with a costly ointment that supposedly will produce the dewy look of a 20-year old.

The saleslady was preaching the standard gospel of our consumer society. The gospel that says you are never good enough. You can never be satisfied with the status quo.

Bummed out at work? Book a cruise. Bored by your sweetheart? Blow the bucks on a new car. Feeling moody and out of sorts? Bag a new outfit.

In a society where the demons of despair run rampant, it's not too surprising that more people visit malls each week than churches. We head to the mall to be delivered from suffering, to be freed from our sins of being too old, too fat, or too weary.

Instead of the chalice, we sip super-sized soft drinks. Instead of sacramental bread, we gobble fast-food burgers.

But who can really blame us? The prophets of consumerism preach their message insistently on the radio, the Internet, and TV. They tell us that the more trinkets we have, the happier we'll be. And if we drive the sleekest car, wear the best cut of shoes and flaunt the costliest jewelry, we'll enter a heavenly kingdom of love and fulfillment—right here on Earth.

Our products reveal our deepest spiritual longings. We drive cars named Infinity. We anoint our limbs with perfumes called Happy, Ecstasy, and Eternity. We scrub our dishes with a soap labeled Joy and wash clothes with Cheer.

But the gospel of consumerism ultimately betrays us. Instead of the resurrection, we get repossession. Instead of finding the messiah, we find ourselves in a financial mess.

That's because what we're seeking doesn't come in a package. It's something all the marketing moguls in the world can't deliver. It's called self-esteem.

Self-esteem is as magical as the first lightning bug of summer. You can't wrap your hands around it, but it's easy to detect. If you have self-esteem, you don't care that your hair is frizzy, limp, or gray. You don't care that your jowls are sagging. That's because you know, deep within, that you're valuable.

Even if you drive a ratty old car and have holes in your shoes. Even if your gas gauge is on empty and your bank balance is nearing zero. Because you're God's child and He cherishes you.

Unfortunately, this message doesn't get much air time. After all, you can't slap self-esteem on a billboard. Or charge it on a card.

But once you experience God's love, you glimpse the wonder of the real kingdom. You can stop prowling through stores seeking happiness. You can stop amassing more trinkets. You can just be yourself. And that's good enough.

17

❖ A Real Turn-Off ❖

"I don't have enough time. I'm too busy. There aren't enough hours in the day."

Sound familiar? When the soup kitchen needs volunteers, or Aunt Molly needs help with home repairs, we'd like to say yes. Too often, though, we sigh and recite a litany of responsibilities.

For most of us, the job easily consumes ten or more hours daily, counting time for dressing, commuting, and "decompressing" once we get home. We're also faced with the countless tasks of everyday life: laundry, meals, grocery shopping, childcare, and housekeeping. Weekends mean church, social gatherings, ferrying Junior to soccer games, and the omnipresent yard work. No wonder the days seem too short.

But a deep pocket of time—about four hours a day—lies untapped in most of our lives.

Look no further than your TV set.

Women, ages 25 to 34, chalk up nearly 32 hours of TV watching a week, while men watch about 28 hours. And kids, ages 6 to 11, are glued to the tube more than 21 hours weekly.

For adults, that's about thirty hours a week when we can't nurture relationships with friends, spouses, and children. Thirty hours a week when we can't help with community and church projects.

Thirty hours when we're "too busy" to play games with our toddlers or help a teen with homework. Thirty hours when we're unavailable to visit Uncle Pete in the nursing home, volunteer at a homeless shelter, serve on a church committee—or pray.

I spent plenty of hours hypnotized by the tube when I was a kid. I grew up in the days when Ed Sullivan and "I Love Lucy" were specialties on the TV menu. The creation of TV dinners and trays was hailed as a lovely way to eat the evening meal without missing one's favorite programs. All too often, mealtime conversations were limited to requests to raise the volume.

Somehow, the presence of a TV in the "living" room seems a sad contradiction. The room reserved for visits from friends and neighbors and for conversations with family members is filled with flickering lights and the drone of electronic voices.

In her book *Heart of Joy,* Mother Teresa emphasized the necessity of caring for the less fortunate. She speculated that on Judgment Day, God wouldn't ask us how many books we had read. It's even more doubtful He'd be impressed by a list of all the sitcoms we've sat through.

In Mother Teresa's shelters for the sick, the dying, and the homeless throughout the world, television sets are conspicuously absent. Removing the TV set frees up time for residents to talk with each other, play games, and participate in life, instead of escaping into an unreal world where the lust for money, power, and sex is portrayed as admirable.

A few years ago, Jef and I turned off our TV for good. The last show we followed faithfully was "Twin Peaks," and as the episodes grew increasingly salacious and violent, we grew increasingly curious about our motivations for continuing to tune in. Could it be we were hooked on television? It seemed a reasonable assumption, given that we had both watched the tube daily since we were small children.

By some estimates, of course, we're missing quite a bit of popular culture. People who open conversations with "Did you see the Dumbo show last night?" probably consider us odd. But we're also missing the insistent brainwashing of commercials that advocate a "more is better" and "you can never have enough" lifestyle.

It would be tempting to blame all of today's social ills on TV viewing, but that, of course, would be a drastic oversimplification. Still, it is worth noting that the average child in the U.S. sees 26,000 celluloid murders by his 18th birthday.

Clearly, kids learn by imitation, and many TV shows depict single parents who juggle parenting, jobs, and dating without any evidence of financial or emotional stress. Pre-marital sex and affairs outside of marriage are accepted as the norm.

The question of whether TV helps create the world we live in— or whether it merely reflects social reality—is easy to answer. If advertisers lacked evidence that TV changes our lives, why would they continue spending billions of dollars to influence our spending behaviors?

18

The Kingdom Called "Enough"

Sometimes I'm enticed by other people's trash.

Not that I'm keen on coffee grounds or eggshells, but over the years I've rescued a cluster of objects destined for burial in a landfill. A snazzy print of the seashore, wind chimes fashioned from silver forks, sturdy desk chairs, and a barbecue grill, to name a few items.

I'm in a quandary though. Although I hate to see perfectly good things going to waste, I'm also hesitant about amassing too much stuff.

St. Benedict, the father of Western monasticism, grappled with similar issues in the sixth century A.D. In his *Rule for Monasteries,* St. Benedict instructed the monks in homespun matters, like clothing, meals, and daily chores, along with loftier concerns like prayer and good works. So many of his words still ring true for people trying to follow Christ today.

Wastefulness was taboo in the monastery, where the monks possessed just enough of everything—two tunics and two cowls each, for example.

"More than that is superfluity," St. Benedict warned.

He'd probably be aghast at the mountains of stuff an average American of the 21st century possesses. He might be floored to learn that we pay rent to store our extras in climate-controlled buildings resembling miniature cities. But in a society dominated by the "more is better" philosophy of consumerism, it's tough to know when you have enough.

When I was a child, my sister and I shared a bedroom. Most houses in our neighborhood had one small bathroom each, and no one felt deprived. Middle-class kids in the U.S. today often have their own rooms and private baths, their own televisions, computers, and cell phones. It's commonplace for homes in trendier sections of Atlanta to sport three or more bathrooms. And don't forget the hot tub.

The story about the miracle of the loaves and fishes reveals Christ's feelings about wastefulness. After feeding the crowd, He instructed the disciples to gather up all the crumbs, "so nothing would be wasted." The disciples gathered twelve baskets of leftovers—and although the gospel account ends there, it's easy to envision what happened next. It's easy to imagine Christ and His friends sharing those baskets with the poor.

St. Benedict, modeling his precepts on the New Testament, strongly emphasized the importance of ministering to the needy. He instructed any monk receiving new clothes to bundle up the old ones for the poor. He also maintained that everything in our lives is a gift from God—a gift to be shared.

The bulging landfills of contemporary Western society no doubt would horrify him. If he were to see how many useable items we discard, he might shudder at our apparent lack of gratitude.

Perhaps St. Benedict would encourage us to recognize how wealthy we are, even if we sometimes feel impoverished. It is a real eye-opener to realize that the vast majority of the world's population lacks cars. Things that we take for granted, like air-conditioning, indoor plumbing, televisions, and computers are major luxuries to most of the world's people.

If we were truly grateful for our possessions, perhaps our longing to stockpile more and more stuff might start to dwindle. And if we were to control our frenzied impulses to buy, buy, buy, perhaps we could dig a little deeper when the collection basket reaches us, especially on days when the collection is slated for the poor.

And maybe one day we might arrive at a sparkling realm of spiritual satisfaction right here on Earth. It's a kingdom St. Benedict evidently knew very well. It's a kingdom called "enough."

Questions for Reflection and Discussion

1. Are you sometimes bothered by all that you own? Is it difficult for you to cut back on buying?

2. Have you ever felt your job was preventing you from serving others?

3. How would your life change if you turned off the T.V.?

4. Why do you go to the mall?

VII

Resurrection

When Mary Magdalene stands sobbing at the empty tomb, the Risen Lord shows up to comfort her.

"Why are you weeping?" He asks her.

How typical that gesture was for Jesus, who couldn't resist taking care of people. His feelings of compassion for the hungry crowd prompted the miracle of the loaves and fishes. Mary and Martha's sorrow over Lazarus' death stirred Him so deeply that He restored their brother to life. And even after His death, He was troubled by Mary Magdalene's grief.

I believe the Risen Lord still visits us. And I believe He makes His presence known in places where people are suffering, especially hospitals and nursing homes.

As a minister to the sick, I occasionally take Holy Communion to Catholic residents at a nursing home a few miles from my house. It was there that I met Lila (not her real name), a red-haired young woman who'd been paralyzed from the neck down following injuries in an automobile accident. After the accident, she and her husband had divorced, and he had gained custody of their two children since Lila could no longer care for them.

When I first met Lila, she didn't seem bitter. She didn't rail against God for her unfathomable losses. Instead, she told me quietly how thankful she was that her children hadn't been injured in the accident. And then she asked me to read aloud from the New Testament.

As I was reading, I glanced up and saw her big eyes fixed on me with such rapt attention that I had the feeling she was listening to a letter from a beloved friend.

Down the hall is another young woman whose life was shattered after a car wreck. Partially paralyzed, Rita (not her real name) suffered severe brain damage and has the halting speech and gestures of a small child. Her mother feeds and bathes her, spends the day by her daughter's side, reading and talking with her, and sleeps at night on a mat on the floor.

The first few times I visited them, Rita would call out to me as I was leaving, but I couldn't understand the excited jumble of words until one day her mom came to my rescue.

"She's saying 'I love you,'" the mother beamed.

Recently Rita's mom asked me for a favor. Her eyes resting on the crucifix in my hand, she asked shyly if I might get her one too, "so I can keep it with me always as a reminder."

At first I was stunned. In the midst of her own terrible suffering, why would she want a reminder of the agony of Christ? And then, of course, I realized I had missed the point. I realized this mother was gazing at the cross, but she was seeing the resurrection.

I suspect that these women in the nursing home have encountered the Risen Lord at the tomb. They know from experience that when we're shuddering with despair, when our hearts are crushed, when the doctors throw their hands up and it seems we have barely a grain of hope left, Jesus speaks our names tenderly.

And then He does what Jesus has always done so well. He stretches out a hand to us. He helps us remove the burial cloths of despair that are constricting our hearts. And as we take His hand, we experience the miracle of the resurrection. We are reborn.

19

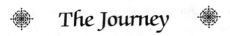 **The Journey**

Her eyes were lit with a mysterious light. Her smile was radiant. But her words baffled me.

"It's hard to explain," she said, "but cancer is a journey."

Mary Anne McKee, a member of my church, had been diagnosed with pancreatic and liver cancer. The doctors had given her a few months to live. Yet here she was at Mass, grinning like someone who'd just won the lottery. She told me excitedly that she'd already outlived the doctors' predictions. She'd enjoyed a lovely Easter. And she'd felt well enough to attend her youngest daughter's high school graduation.

"From now on, the rest is gravy," she smiled.

I imagined myself in her shoes and I couldn't see myself smiling. She seemed to have tapped into some secret spring of strength that was entirely foreign to me.

About a month later, my life took a completely unexpected detour when I found myself joining the ranks of the thousands of people each year whose medical charts are branded with the word "cancer." Mary Anne was sympathetic and compassionate when she learned of my illness. She promised to pray for me, and she invited me to a cancer support group at a nearby hospital.

"I don't know how I'd manage without the group," she enthused.

Then she told me more about her journey. When she had first been diagnosed, she'd sought counseling at the hospital.

"All I did was cry during the first few sessions," she confided. "It took a long time before I dared to wear mascara."

Still, the next time I saw her in church she was wearing mascara. Somehow she had emerged from her dark cranny of grief.

I started praying for Mary Anne the day I learned of her illness. I continued every day for the next few months. Once, while praying for her at Mass, I turned around and saw her a few pews behind me. Her head was bent in prayer. The hair she had lost from the chemotherapy treatments was now growing back. It was wispy and white.

Our eyes met and she smiled. At that moment, I didn't understand the joy she radiated, but I envied it.

One night, I went to the support group with her. When we entered the room, the people sitting in the circle looked up expectantly. Some were wearing wigs to conceal their hair loss from chemotherapy. Some were thin and pale. But they all managed a smile when they saw Mary Anne.

With great excitement, she announced her good news. The latest tests had revealed that the lesions in her liver were starting to heal. As everyone applauded, the room hummed with love.

As the weeks passed, I continued praying for Mary Anne, envisioning how her eyes had gleamed when she'd shared her good news.

And then one day in church, I heard the announcement from the pulpit. "Mary Anne McKee died earlier this week. Please remember her in your prayers."

My heart dropped. Despite her enthusiasm, despite her fierce faith, she had become another grim statistic.

"It isn't fair," I thought tearfully. "She had so much to live for. She was only in her forties." And, of course, the next thought was predictable enough: "Someday they'll read my name."

And of course they will.

My prayer is that I'll have lived as fully as Mary Anne did. Shortly before her death, she attended her parents' 50th anniversary celebration. Then she and her husband went on a camping trip.

Mary Anne is still in my thoughts every night as I lie in bed. But now, instead of praying for her health, I'm asking her to put in a good word for me with the Lord. I envision her grinning mischievously at me. And I can almost hear her assuring me, "The journey is over. And now the rest is gravy."

20

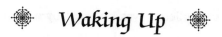 *Waking Up*

When I was in my twenties, I witnessed my mother's slow, agonizing decline from breast cancer. After her death, with all the arrogance of youth, I vowed I wouldn't suffer the same fate. Devoting myself to a vigorous quest for perfect health, I jogged daily, downed fistfuls of vitamins, and shunned red meat and fatty foods.

My cholesterol levels were perfect, my weight just right. My doctors marveled at my blood pressure readings. But the fact that I was the daughter of a woman who'd succumbed to breast cancer was duly noted on my chart. And whenever a new doctor learned of my family history, he somberly shook his head.

When my worst nightmare came true, and I was diagnosed with cancer, friends and family poured out their love. Boxes of chocolates, heady clusters of gardenias, loaves of homemade bread crowded the front porch. There were hugs, tears, and prayers.

At first, I lived on automatic pilot. I watered the garden, went grocery shopping, and paid the bills. I fed the cat and washed the dishes. But by late afternoon each day, a fist of grief would suddenly squeeze my heart. I'd have to drop whatever I was doing and plant myself on the couch—and weep.

Once the weeping subsided, I was gripped by another wave of emotion. It was denial. Even after I saw the lab report with the words "breast cancer" in black and white, I still refused to believe the diagnosis. Surely, I thought, there was some mix-up in the lab. Surely the doctor would call any moment to tell me I was fine.

When he never called, I was buffeted by a storm of anger. My passionate quest for health had clearly failed. Despite the tofu, despite the purified water, despite the high-fiber foods, I was on my way to becoming just another depressing statistic. What a fool I've been, I fumed.

After the surgery, there finally was good news. The tumor was small and had been discovered early, the surgeon explained kindly. My condition was treatable. Still, even as I was flooded with relief, tentacles of sorrow would grip my heart now and again. I felt like I was bidding farewell to a beloved friend. An old version of myself, carefree and healthy.

That was two months ago. Now, as the days pass, I'm starting to notice some glimmers of light in the midst of the storm. It may seem ludicrous to suggest that something good might come from cancer, but I've discovered it can be the greatest wake-up call of your life.

When you come nose to nose with the Grim Reaper, your whole perspective changes. Suddenly you acknowledge you won't be here forever. Suddenly you have a fierce determination to squeeze every drop of juice from the time you have left. And you start asking yourself the big questions. Am I on the right path? Am I doing whatever tasks God put me on this planet to perform? Or am I running like a gerbil on a wheel, too frantic and exhausted to reflect on my purpose?

The old saying, "You can't take it with you," is only partially true. If you mean stock options and fancy cars, I agree wholeheartedly. But I believe there is something you take with you—and something you leave behind—after your life is over. It's love.

No one will recall that we wore designer clothes or costly cologne. You never hear someone saying, "How I miss Aunt Erma. She had the finest jewelry and most luxurious furniture." Instead, what you hear all the time is, "She had such a big heart. She was such a good friend."

The lessons I'm learning from cancer are all about love. I've realized that the generous impulses that pop into our minds, seemingly from nowhere, really are little directives from God. Before my diagnosis, I sometimes would envision myself cutting roses from the garden for a friend, just to show my affection. But so often I squelched my impulses.

"Maybe I'm going overboard," I'd fret.

Now, when a generous impulse pops into my mind, I try to heed it. Sometimes when I'm out shopping, I'll spot a woman in a pretty dress. But she looks troubled. Her face is sad.

"That's a lovely dress," I'll say, and her face will magically light up.

It's such a small gesture, but as Mother Teresa once reminded us, little acts of kindness are like drops in the ocean. Without each drop, the ocean would disappear.

One day recently, I envisioned myself baking cookies to share with other patients at the clinic where I go for radiation therapy. In the old days, I would have talked myself out of it.

"Why go to such trouble for strangers?" I might have said.

Instead, I baked the cookies and then placed them by the coffee pot in the clinic. A few moments later, I heard the aluminum foil crinkling. I looked up from where I was sitting and spotted six cancer patients munching on cookies. And they were smiling.

If I had the power to rewrite the script of my life, I'd strike out the part about cancer. I'd remove the scars from my body and give myself a glowing bill of health. But there's one part of the script I wouldn't strike out. It's that wake-up call. The part about the lessons I'm learning. The part about love.

Questions for Reflection and Discussion

1. How have difficult times affected your faith?

2. What are some moments of "rebirth" or "awakenings" in your life?

3. How would you like to be remembered after you're gone?

VIII

Serving

I dreamt I was standing at the pearly gates, clutching a handful of coupons.

"What are those?" St. Peter asked.

"My volunteering coupons," I replied, placing them in his hand.

Then I explained how I'd earned them. All the times I'd pitched in at church—answering phones, singing in the choir, volunteering to help at the AIDS home, and visiting shut-ins.

My dream took a detour when St. Peter suddenly handed the coupons back.

"You've got it all wrong, my love," he said gently. "You can't buy your way into heaven."

I was about to protest when the alarm clock shrieked and I awoke.

I was a little bit miffed. It hasn't exactly been a picnic chalking up spiritual brownie points. For one thing, no matter how big your stash may be, you always run into someone who has more.

My friend, the mother of two young girls, recently volunteered to oversee our church's bazaar and flea market. She also visits nursing homes, organizes the children's liturgy, takes elderly people to medical appointments, and volunteers at her kids' school.

Just envisioning her stack of coupons exhausts me.

I worked hard at being a straight-A Christian as a kid. In my fervor to follow the Church's rules, I showed up every Saturday without fail at the confessional. I had a very slim grasp of numerical theory, so I couched all my sins the same way.

"I disobeyed my mom one hundred times," I announced. "And fought with my sister—one hundred times."

To his credit, the priest didn't emit even one snicker.

I went to Holy Communion every Sunday, carefully fasting for the appropriate amount of time beforehand. I prayed fervently for the living and the dead, including my deceased pet turtles, Wormy and Flat-Top.

Then I blew it. My report cards studded with gold stars went up in flames when I trundled off to college, leaving behind my stuffed animals, my creaky old bike—and my Bible. Saying prayers and going to church went out the window the day I opened a philosophy book and discovered the brave new world of atheism.

"Atheism is cool," I thought. "If there's no God, you can throw out the rules and regulations. No more sins. No more sermons. No more penance. Let the party begin!"

The party went on for over twenty years. Finally, sporting a massive spiritual hangover, I returned to my childhood faith.

The rules had relaxed. The priest faced the congregation and spoke English instead of Latin. Women no longer covered their heads in church. The fast before Communion had been shortened.

It wasn't long, however, before my coupon fetish reared its head again. But there was a new twist. Instead of scoring spiritual points for toeing the lines, I began awarding them to myself for serving the less fortunate.

If I put $30 in the collection basket for the poor, I chalked up a generosity coupon. If I visited someone at the hospital, I grabbed bonus points for compassion.

The notion of unmerited love was foreign to me. The idea that God might love me just for myself was a bit too much to handle. Impossible to believe someone might love you even if you slept through Mass and got straight F's in school.

Then, one day, I remembered the story of the thief dying on the cross next to Jesus. Bleeding, sweating, and crying, the man had little to show for his life. And he asked for so little: "Jesus, remember me when you come into your kingdom" (Luke 23:42).

That's all. Remember me. Don't forget me. Keep me in mind. The same stuff we say when we're applying for a job and we know we lack the credentials. As we shuffle out the door, we murmur, "Keep me in my mind if something turns up."

Christ did not reply: "You may enter my kingdom if you can prove you tithed, attended the synagogue, and ministered to your fellow man."

Evidently He recognized the man's sincerity—and desperation—and that was enough. Then He uttered the words that surely were a balm to that tortured soul: "Today you will be with me in Paradise" (Luke 23:43).

Today. Not tomorrow or next week. Not after you've done time for your sins. Not after you've made amends for your life. Right now.

I dreamt about St. Peter again last night. This time, he took me on a tour. I saw a huge banquet table. A real celebration. A true feast. And there was a sign over the table: "All you can eat. Come as you are. And it's all free."

As I danced joyfully through the pearly gates, I discovered a secret. They had been open all along.

21

 One of the Flock

The first time I saw our pastor blessing parishioners who were called "extraordinary ministers," I felt a jolt of energy zip up and down my back.

"That's for me," I thought.

Taking Holy Communion to the elderly and the ailing seemed a perfect way to follow in the footsteps of the Good Shepherd.

Since that day years ago, I've visited an assortment of Christ's sheep. Some have been at home recuperating from surgery or illnesses. Some have been frail and living in nursing homes. A few have rallied and now attend Sunday Mass again. Two have died.

For over a year, I've been visiting three women in their eighties. Mary, Agnes, and Anne—whom I call "my ladies"—live in high-rise condominiums near my home. Widows, they suffer from a variety of ailments, ranging from diabetes and arthritis to heart disease and cancer.

We meet Sunday afternoons in Agnes' condo, sitting in over-stuffed chairs under the watchful eyes of her collection of china dolls. When we first settle down, my ladies unleash a stream of chatter about their children, their grandchildren, favorite TV shows, new recipes.

After a while, Mary says, "Let's go to church."

Our altar is a coffee table, upon which I place a linen cloth, a crucifix, and a small golden pyx, which contains the consecrated hosts. Our communion service is an abbreviated version of the Mass, which opens with the greeting, "Peace be with you," proceeds through prayers, a gospel reading, and the Lord's Prayer.

Finally, there is my favorite moment, when I raise the host and declare, "This is the Lamb of God who takes away the sins of the world. Happy are those who are called to this supper."

I love tending to my ladies. Even if Christ hadn't encouraged Peter to feed His sheep, I think I might have done it anyway, because this little flock is so kind and grateful. But when I became ill last year, everything changed. Suddenly the stress and turmoil of my illness drained me of energy and I didn't feel capable of caring for anyone but myself.

When I called Mary to tell her about my dilemma, I cried. She listened quietly and reassured me, and she promised she would tell the other ladies.

After a few months, I mustered up enough energy to visit my ladies again. Despite my weight loss and somewhat bedraggled appearance, they assured me I looked beautiful. I knew they were stretching the truth, but it didn't matter. Like a child, I basked in the light of their love.

During the communion service that day, I asked them for prayer requests, as I always did. We usually prayed for their children and grandchildren, the repose of their husbands' souls, and the health of their friends.

That day, Agnes chimed in, "Let's pray for *you*, baby."

And as my ladies bowed their heads in prayer, I was moved to tears, remembering the words of Christ who encouraged us to feed His sheep as a way to show our love for God.

Bowing my head, I thanked God I was able to care for my ladies. And I thanked Him for something else that day, something the Good Shepherd hadn't mentioned—but surely would understand.

Sometimes, without warning, the tables turn on us. And when that happened to me, I discovered something. Although it's a great blessing to be a shepherd, it's also rather lovely being counted among the flock.

22

✸ Turning Doris ✸

A woman is hidden behind the white shower curtain. Judging by the sounds, I assume she's soaping herself.

Today's my first day volunteering at the Gift of Grace, a home where Mother Teresa's nuns and volunteers care for poor women with AIDS. When I arrived earlier this morning, I asked an experienced volunteer named Iris for a broom. Then I felt moved to explain that I want to start out doing housework and eventually try my hand at patient care.

"It's not that I'm afraid of getting AIDS," I emphasized. "It's just that I'm a bit clumsy and have never worked around very sick people."

Iris said nothing but nodded compassionately.

It's taken me a while to pick up this broom. When Mother Teresa first sent four nuns to Atlanta a few years ago, Jef and I helped the sisters transform a rundown house into a sparkling home. Since then, my volunteer efforts have consisted in taking the healthier residents shopping.

But I've been eager to move up a rung or two on the volunteering ladder, which means pushing myself to do what's really tough. And for me that means working inside the house with the very ill residents.

Moments ago, one of the little nuns shyly asked me to help the woman in the shower, so I've put down my broom and taken up my post in the bathroom. When the woman suddenly draws back the curtain, I'm startled to see her, emaciated, naked, and trembling, and holding on to a towel rack for dear life. She appears to be waiting for me to do something. When I hesitate, she asks, "Would you dry my back?"

I grab a nearby towel and begin, rather gingerly, to dry her back. Thoughts fill my mind like birds darkening a sky. I've never dried the back of another woman and it's been years since I towel-dried a baby. Maybe that's why my gestures seem hopelessly clumsy. After all, I've never touched a person who is dying.

When my mother was dying from cancer more than twenty years ago, I wasn't there to help her as she plummeted into the final stages of her illness. Instead, I was in college 300 miles away, where I somehow managed to delude myself about the seriousness of her illness.

I'm wearing protective gloves, but an icy current of fear still courses through my soul as the towel moves downward over the woman's rump, her thighs, her legs.

My thoughts run to Iris. Even though I met her only a half hour ago, I've already gleaned important information about her. She's a massage therapist. She's a mother. When her mother was dying, Iris was there to care for her. Iris is the kind of woman you know you can lean on in an emergency.

So when the woman in the shower asks me for help putting on a diaper, I know just what to do. I call for Iris.

She's there in seconds. I don't bore her with my excuses — how it's been years since I've diapered a baby and I can barely remember the procedure. I don't mention the fear that keeps bubbling upwards from some deep, unknown part of me.

Iris rescues me cheerfully. One, two, three, the diaper is on. Next she helps the woman out of the shower and into a wheel chair. Naked except for the pale blue diaper, the woman seems to radiate light as she settles into the chair. Her head is wreathed in foam rubber hair rollers and around her neck she wears sparkling, ice-blue rosary beads and shiny medals of the Blessed Virgin Mary.

Now another tiny nun wearing the familiar blue-and-white sari of Mother Teresa's order walks into the bathroom and flashes us a big crescent of a smile.

"How are you today?" she asks in a voice thick with the cadences of India.

"I'm alive, thanks be to God," proclaims the woman with an even bigger smile.

Now Sister turns to me.

"Lorraine, will you help me turn Doris over in bed?"

Iris mentioned earlier that Doris—"rigid as a board"—is in the last stages of AIDS.

All I can think is: "Oh, God, I'm not ready. I came here today to sweep."

The words that spill from my mouth are simple: "Sister, I'm not ready."

No doubt Sister has seen this reaction hundreds of times.

"It's OK," she says and then rushes off.

I feel like I've failed some important test, but I'm not sure who's grading it. I know I've missed my chance to learn something important. Not just how to turn someone in bed but also how to take the next step in confronting my horror of AIDS—and of death itself.

Somewhat dejectedly, I take the broom and start going from room to room. In one of the rooms, a black cheery woman in her sixties is making her bed. Smiling at me with slightly oversized false teeth, she points proudly to a photo of a tiny girl decked out in a ruffled pink dress.

"My granchile," she says proudly, and I remark over the loveliness of the child. Then the woman grows serious.

"Sister want me to move down the hall to another room," she says. "But I don't want to. Four people's died in that room. It ain't that I'm afraid of death, no, I'm just afraid of that room."

As I continue sweeping, I realize this woman has cut to the chase. Am I afraid of getting AIDS and dying or am I afraid of death in general—or what? Is the woman fooling herself about her feelings about the room? Am I deluding myself about my own fears?

My reflections don't have time to simmer very long. From room to room I go, sweeping, sweeping, sweeping. Soon I'm in Doris' room. Still and small beneath the covers, with just the top of her head showing, she reminds me of a leaf that the slightest breeze might lift away. Carefully, I sweep around her bed, praying her death won't be too agonizing. And I pray for myself too: "Lord, help me get to the point where I can say 'yes' to turning Doris."

The next day at Mass the priest quotes a passage that Mother Teresa loved: "I was hungry and you gave me food, I was thirsty and you gave me something to drink . . . I was sick and you took care of me" (Matthew 25:35-36).

Of course, now I have to face it. In refusing to help the sisters with Doris, I turned my back on Christ.

That night, though, as I toss uncomfortably in bed, I finally uncover the real problem. The truth is that Christ's words aren't rooted in my heart. How can I reject Christ when I haven't fully embraced Him?

Yes, I know in a dry intellectual way from the books I've read that Mother Teresa encountered Jesus in the dying poor. And I comprehend the literal meaning of Christ's words in the passage in Matthew. But somehow I feel I've been trying to nibble on the leftovers of someone else's mystical feast.

I recall a passage in *Song of the Bird* by Anthony de Mello. He had a good relationship with the Lord, de Mello writes, but he always had an uncomfortable sensation that the Lord wanted him to look at Him. De Mello refused. He was afraid he would encounter an accusation of some unrepented sin.

One day, de Mello summoned up his courage and finally looked. And what he saw surprised him.

"There was no accusation," he writes. "There was no demand. The eyes just said, 'I love you.' And I walked out and, like Peter, I wept."

Doris died a week ago after being tenderly cared for by the sisters and volunteers. Although I never spoke with her, I cherish the lesson she taught me.

Until I can feel God's love for me on a deep, soulful level—love that exists whether I "prove myself" or not through volunteer work—I'll just be going through the motions. I'll be trying to score extra credit points on an exam I can't pass.

I hope that Doris is now praying for me. Praying that I'll learn to accept myself as the person behind the broom, rather than at the bedside—but the one He loves just the same.

23

 Pirates and Pelicans

When Jef and I first started vacationing on Cedar Key, I fell prey to some tempting clichés about paradise as we sampled the seemingly endless joys of our newly discovered Margaritaville. I felt that we were riding a high tide that would last forever.

As we've become more familiar with the little town, though, we've glimpsed some of the inevitable flaws of island life, like the beatings endured by Mother Nature as a result of mankind's relentless urge to have fun.

Some of the rescued manatees at nearby Homosassa Springs bear ugly scars on their backs attesting to man's love affair with speed boats. They're the lucky ones; many of the endangered animals perish after a lashing by a boat's propeller blades.

The birds also bear the brunt of human encroachment, when habitats are destroyed to make room for human dwelling places. And some island birds, especially the pelicans, run the risk of getting injured by discarded fishing hooks and lines.

Fortunately, there are compassionate people who tend to the injured birds. A man known as the "Bird Man of Cedar Key" is one of these.

Jef and I first encountered the Bird Man one evening when we were sitting on the edge of the Big Dock beholding a rousing sunset. Near us was a solitary fisherman who had a large pelican keeping him company. With a wild-looking beard, long, unkempt hair, and well-worn clothing faded from the sun, the man reminded me of a storybook version of a pirate.

As the pelican inched closer to the man, like a hound dog positioning himself to beg for a bone, I half expected the gruff-looking guy to shoo the bird away. Instead, the two remained sitting side by side like old friends at a bar.

Suddenly we heard a commotion on the lower dock. A great flapping of wings in the waters below signaled that a pelican had been hooked by a fishing line. Looking down, we saw the bird fluttering helplessly in the water, trying to free himself, but only getting more and more tangled.

The pirate grabbed a long-handled net and rushed to the lower dock. Just before he arrived on the scene, however, the fisherman cut the line and the panicked bird, hook imbedded in his flesh, flew away, dragging the rest of the line with him.

The pirate, net in hand, stalked angrily back to his original spot on the dock. He was muttering under his breath.

"The bird hasn't got any brains," he said, when he noticed me looking at him. "It'll go and hang itself from a tree. Those people should know better!"

The next night another splendid sunset enticed us to the Big Dock. In the distance we spotted cormorants sitting on markers and drying their wings, silhouetted against the fiery sky like black angels. Pelicans were parading up and down the dock, their beady eyes hungrily fixed on the fishermen, who might at any moment toss one of the smaller fish their way. Our pirate was nowhere to be seen.

I noticed a good-sized pelican standing apart from the other birds, wings stretched out awkwardly. Looking closer, I saw a hook and line dangling from beneath one of its wings, the hook firmly imbedded in the poor bird's flesh. Cringing, I wondered how long the bird had been suffering. I dashed over to the nearby bait shop, hoping to get advice from the owner.

"A pelican has a hook caught in it," I blurted out.

His response was quick. "Try the Bird Man. He was just outside a minute ago."

Rushing outside, I saw the pirate from the night before, leaning nonchalantly against a car. When I explained the dilemma, he moved swiftly, opening the car trunk and removing a fishing pole.

Was he planning to go fishing at a time like this? I wondered.

As if reading my mind, he said, "I'll have to catch a fish to attract the bird."

We hurried back to the dock where I pointed out the injured bird. Once the Bird Man spotted the pelican, he evidently changed his mind about fishing, instead accepting a small fish from a nearby fisherman.

He quietly offered the fish to the bird, who edged cautiously closer to grab the treat. When the pelican was close enough, he gently but firmly grasped its beak and then straddled the bird, murmuring words of encouragement all the while.

He worked with the deftness of a surgeon, unfolding the big wing to reveal the imbedded hook, then using wire clippers to snip off the barb.

"We've been through this before, haven't we, baby?" he said as he carefully removed the rest of the hook.

The bird had stopped struggling and sat quietly while he worked, perhaps sensing that his intentions were peaceful.

Once he had removed the hook, the man examined the pelican's mouth and then felt along its stomach to be sure no other hooks were lodged there. Then he released the pelican and we watched it gratefully totter away.

Over the years, visits with the Bird Man have become part of our island routine. Sometimes we see him near the water's edge hauling buckets of fish to feed the pelicans that eagerly surround him. Often he tells us about the problems the birds face on an island that's becoming steadily more developed.

Some folks have saluted his efforts to help the birds, while others, put off by his scraggly appearance and eccentric ways, poke fun at him.

It's clear the Bird Man has found his calling on this tiny piece of land in the middle of the Gulf of Mexico. Even if he can't rescue every bird that needs help, his efforts make a difference.

He doesn't drive a sporty vehicle or wear trendy clothes. Instead, he tools around on a motor scooter attached to a small trailer filled with bird-rescue paraphernalia. But the birds don't mind.

He lives in an old trailer park instead of a fancy house. But the birds don't mind. Unlike humans, they're not impressed by what a person owns or how much money he has.

That's the remarkable thing about animals. They don't care a minnow for appearances, and the elaborate trappings of wealth and power do not impress them. But they can sense a compassionate heart a mile away.

Questions for Reflection and Discussion

1. How has "feeding God's sheep" changed you?

2. What ministries do you feel called to?

3. How do people like "the Bird Man of Cedar Key" serve God?

4. Is it easy for you to accept, on a deep, soulful level, that God's love doesn't depend on your doing good works?

IX

Denying

In the gospels, a rooster crows three times, punctuating Peter's passionate denials that he ever knew a man named Jesus.

It's hard to condemn Peter for trying to distance himself from a friend who is facing the horrible death of crucifixion. We're all like Peter. Maybe our denials aren't quite so dramatic, but we all turn our backs on Christ in our everyday lives.

Maybe we're at a party where someone mocks Christianity, and we remain silent. Maybe we fear being branded as a fanatic. Or as politically incorrect.

Maybe we tell ourselves that we believe in Christ, but we deny the messages of the gospels.

"Christ couldn't have meant *that*," we think, when we come to a particularly demanding passage.

He couldn't have been serious when He said we should sell everything and follow him. He must have been joking when He recommended turning the other cheek and giving no thought to the morrow.

He told us how hard it would be for a rich man to enter heaven, yet we work overtime at the office, trying to amass a fortune. He said the poor would be blessed, but how often we despise poor people. We pay homage instead to wealthy politicians, rock stars, and athletes.

He said the meek would inherit the earth, but we shun a wimpy foreign policy, instead supporting politicians whose aggressive policies often result in the mass destruction of our fellow man.

He recommended that we seek God in strangers, yet we shun the desperate people who cross our borders without the proper papers. We label them "illegal aliens."

He cherished children, who were precious to Him, yet we live in a world where the widespread destruction of millions of infants in the womb is commonplace.

He forgave the men who brutalized Him and nailed Him to the cross. Still, we murmur about an "eye for an eye" and applaud the state for destroying convicted killers.

He promised us life beyond the grave, but we're terrified at the prospects of aging and dying. We have handy euphemisms to describe old people—"golden-agers, seniors, the elderly"—and other expressions that soften the reality of death.

"She passed away; he was laid to rest," we murmur.

We fail Jesus over and over again, just like the disciples did. He asked them to pray with Him in the Garden of Gethsemane, and they fell asleep. He told them countless times to stop being afraid, yet after His death they were terrified, huddled behind locked doors.

The first time God appeared on Earth, He was disguised as a helpless infant born to a young couple who lived in poverty. If He were to show up on Earth today, He might surprise us again, with an equally unimpressive resumé.

Perhaps He'd be a down-and-out homeless guy in a shabby suit. Or a desperately lonely woman behind bars. Maybe He'd be handicapped or deformed.

I wonder what our reactions would be. Would we turn our backs on Him and label Him a beggar, a loser, a nothing? And would we be shocked to hear the cock crowing?

24

 No Vacancy for Satan

Satan has always been a globe-trotter.

In the Book of Job, God asks Satan where he's been lately.

"Roaming the earth, and patrolling it," is the chilling reply.

And you can bet he's chalking up frequent-flyer miles today. But don't expect a little fellow in a red suit to swoop through your window. He's much more subtle.

Sometimes you sit bolt upright at 3 a.m. You feel like you're bobbing in a sea of fear. Then you know he's paying a call. And he totes such a deep bag of tricks. He lures us to the abyss of worrying and nudges us off the edge.

When I was a child, the 3 a.m. worries were simple enough. "What if I fail the math test?" "What if I don't make friends at school?"

In my twenties, my fears escalated. "What if my boyfriend leaves me?" "What if my mother dies?"

I failed a few math tests, my boyfriend did leave me—and one day, my beloved mother died. But in some mysterious way those wounds eventually healed and life went on.

Christ knew all about Satan's tricks. That's why He said time and again: "Fear not. Do not let your hearts be troubled. Don't worry about tomorrow."

We may follow that sage advice in the light of day, but when darkness seeps into the house, old habits sometimes ensnare us.

"What if I lose my job?" "What if the lab report is positive?" "What if the teachers can't teach Johnny to read?"

The devil seems to sense our vulnerability. It's no wonder he showed up in the desert after Christ's forty-day fast. He knew the Lord was hungry, so Satan started off with the basics.

"Command these stones to become loaves of bread," he sneered (Matthew 4:3).

When Christ refused, the devil upped the ante. He offered Christ power over all the kingdoms of the world. A very tempting package. One that many politicians today would be hard-pressed to resist.

But there was a long string attached. The devil wanted to be worshiped. And when Christ roared, "Away with you, Satan," the horned one exited quickly.

The prince of darkness still yearns to be worshiped today. He still creeps into the desert of our hearts. And he's very crafty. He wraps sins in nice boxes with frilly ribbons and dangles them before us.

His suggestions seem quite reasonable. Quite trendy. Quite in keeping with the lifestyles of our modern-day saints, the rich and famous CEOs, movie stars, rock idols.

Suddenly we start pondering ways to outdo our neighbor. Maybe we'll buy a fancier car or a bigger house. Suddenly we start believing it's fine to crush toes as we scurry up the corporate ladder. It's fine to two-time our sweetheart. You can almost hear Satan howling in delight.

He also lures us with self-doubts. In his book *Job and the Mystery of Suffering*, Richard Rohr describes Satan as the "negative voices that assault people . . . and tell them they are unacceptable, stupid, not good enough."

You've probably heard those voices. They say you're not skilled enough to get the job. Not attractive enough to find a mate. Not smart enough to make the grade.

Fortunately there's an antidote to this fearful spiritual virus. As St. John told us, "Perfect love casts out fear" (1 John 4:18).

That means love for our neighbor, even the guy in the next cubicle. Love for our spouse, even if she's plumper and grayer than the person we married 25 years ago. And compassion for ourselves, especially when we're haunted by self-doubts.

Maybe we can't entirely banish Satan from the Earth. But maybe we can cancel the old globe-trotter's 3 a.m. reservation. We can hang up a "no vacancy" sign in our hearts. And send him packing.

25

 Fearful Encounters

I peeked into the room. It was quite crowded. Many people were checking their watches as if they were expecting someone.

I took a deep breath before opening the door. I'm the one they're expecting, I realized. I'd called the meeting, and I was nervous.

There were men and women, young and old, well-dressed and shabby. But I recognized them immediately.

They were my worst fears.

The room grew quiet as I took my seat. A big guy was hunched over in his chair near the window. I decided to start with him.

"How long have you been with me?" I asked him.

"I came on board when you were just a little kid," he said, adjusting his tie.

"And you are . . . ?"

"I'm your fear of being abandoned."

Suddenly I remembered the babysitters that had paraded through our house after my mom had gone back to work when I was just two years old. Every time she'd walked out the door, my sister and I had wailed. We had feared she wouldn't return.

"Aren't you somewhat outdated?" I wondered aloud. "My mom's been dead for years."

"Oh, I keep up with the times," he replied. "You never know when your husband might walk out on you."

"That's absurd," I countered. "We've been happily married for nearly twenty years."

He glowered at me. "Call me absurd if you want to. You're the boss."

I stalled for time, jotting down notes while I reflected. I have a loving husband, a family, good friends. Why is this guy still on the payroll, I wondered.

I glanced around the room again. I spotted a snappily dressed woman who looked eager to talk.

"Who are you?" I asked.

"Your fear of dying," she said in a proud tone of voice. "I've been with you ever since your mom died of breast cancer over twenty years ago."

She gestured at a well-heeled woman sitting behind her. "She reports to me," she said. "She's your fear of suffering."

"I work really hard and I put in long hours," she added. "I think I deserve a raise."

I had to agree with her. She certainly seemed to be working overtime lately. Ever since I'd been diagnosed with cancer, she'd been paying me visits first thing in the morning and last thing at night. I certainly couldn't accuse her of slacking off.

Still, I felt ashamed to acknowledge her identity. She made me uneasy. If I truly believed that this world is transitory, a way station between birth and eternity, then surely I wouldn't perceive death as such a terrible thing.

Stirring from my reflections, I realized that I'd nearly overlooked someone. He was the tallest guy in the room. He looked miffed as he raised a beefy hand.

"I'm one of your main fears," he said. "I underpin all the others. Without me, the rest would be nothing."

He paused and then delivered the punch line.

"I'm your fear that the promises of Christ are false. I'm your fear that when you die, you will confront total nothingness."

A hush fell over the room. Everyone looked at me, but I was too stunned to reply. I couldn't really deny what he'd said. If I truly believed in the Lord's teachings, I certainly wouldn't be confronting a roomful of fears. Didn't Christ say, over and over, "Fear not" and "Don't let your hearts be troubled"? Wasn't He always saying, "Peace be with you"?

At that moment, I spotted someone sitting all by himself in a corner. He looked different from the rest. He had very big, soulful eyes.

"Which fear are you?" I asked.

"I'm not a fear," he said quietly. "I sneaked into the meeting out of curiosity. You see, I represent hundreds of others who aren't here right now. I stand for all the prayers that have been said for you during the past year, and all the prayers still being said for you by your friends, your church community, your family, your readers."

He reached out his hand and I grasped it gently. As his fingers intertwined with mine, I felt my anxiety starting to ebb.

Suddenly there was an ugly sound of snarling and growling. Looking up, I saw the fears rising from their seats. Horrified, I realized they were heading straight for us.

Mouth dry, heart pounding, I did the only thing I knew how to do. I tightened my grip on the gentle guy's hand and closed my eyes. Then I began to pray aloud: "Our Father, who art in heaven."

And when I looked up, the fears had vanished.

Questions for Reflection and Discussion

1. What causes you to deny Christ and how do you feel later?

2. What are some of your 3 a.m. worries? Did you ever connect them to Satan?

3. If you called a meeting of your worst fears, how would they introduce themselves?

X

Grace

When my mom was growing up in Greenwich Village in the 1920s, her name plagued her. An awkward, painfully shy child, she was the brunt of jokes by children who loved pointing out the discrepancy between her demeanor and her name.

Her name was Grace.

When she told me the sad tales of her childhood, I had difficulty imagining her as the object of anyone's scorn. In my eyes she was the most beautiful—and graceful—woman in the world. And I was proud she had chosen Grace as my middle name.

Still, I was somewhat confused about grace. I wondered how my name was connected with our family's blessing each night at supper.

"Let's say grace," my mom would chirp, and then we'd all make the sign of the cross and chant in unison, "Bless us, O Lord, and these thy gifts, which we are about to receive from thy bounty. . . . "

When the nuns at school taught me the "Hail Mary," we addressed the Blessed Mother as someone "full of grace." Whispering those words, I pictured a chalice overflowing with a glowing beverage. I didn't know exactly what the beverage was, but I knew it was special, because Mary was.

The nuns explained that God poured grace into our hearts when we went to confession or received Holy Communion. I marveled as I pictured a sweet balm drenching the big white disk that was my soul.

I still marvel over grace today.

"What is grace?" I asked a theology professor one day as he passed my desk in the library.

He paused for a moment. Then he looked out the window and smiled at a redbud tree ablaze with blooms.

"Paying attention," he said.

Checking the dictionary, I learned that grace comes from the Latin, *gratia*, meaning a pleasing quality, favor, and thanks. The word has many meanings: charm of form; thoughtfulness toward others; a temporary exemption—a grace period—and a blessing at meals.

Grace is the unmerited love and favor of God toward mankind, Webster says. It is God's way of strengthening us morally.

I like the notion that grace is unmerited. We don't have to pass any tests or perform any tricks. God tips over a pitcher of love—and we open our hearts to receive it.

On my evening walks, I often visit a spindly-legged cat that lives on the next block. When she spots me at a distance coming up the street, she runs to greet me, her toenails clicking delightedly against the pavement. Then she rolls on the ground and lets me rub her back, while she rumbles in gratitude.

Perhaps such soulful moments are everywhere, if we just look. Perhaps each moment of the day can glisten with such grace.

I confess I have a tendency to dwell on the valleys where grace seems lacking, rather than on the peaks where it shimmers.

But I'm trying to notice the divine touches that embellish an ordinary day. Roses exploding into flames of color, seeming to shout "Hallelujah!" as they point at the sun. A sky laced with white-frosting clouds. And the mysterious music of owls calling to their mates at night.

"Dear God," I whisper at night, "thank you for the graces. Help me to see your gifts in every moment of every day. Help me to be like the little cat. Help me to pay attention."

26

 Mother Teresa and the Manatees

As a child, I embraced Catholicism with all its trimmings. Rosary beads, saints, and novenas were as familiar as jumping rope and playing hopscotch.

But when I went away to college at age 17, I encountered the world of atheism for the first time. Having digested Marx's claim that religion was the opiate of the people and Freud's theory that believing in God was merely wish fulfillment, I felt the grounding of my faith crumbling. Praying was mere superstition, I soon concluded, tossing my rosary beads and prayer cards into a dresser drawer. By graduation day, I was a full-blown atheist.

They say there are no atheists in foxholes, and I'll venture a guess that there are few atheists sitting at the bedside of a loved one who is dying. And so, a few years later, when my mom was stricken with cancer, I dredged up a few kernels of faith and tried to strike a deal with the God I had abandoned.

"If you cure her, I'll come back to you," I vowed.

Sadly, the deal fell through. On the day of our mother's death, my sister confided in hushed tones that a mysterious aroma of roses had permeated her house. Although I knew that the scent of roses was supposedly connected with the presence of the Blessed Virgin Mary, I was so bitter that I dismissed my sister's report as a sign of emotional duress. I turned my back on God for the next decade.

Reflecting on those years now, I think God nudged me many times to return to Him, but I was too stubborn — until it became impossible to ignore Him any longer.

One day, Jef and I were on vacation in Florida, lunching in our tiny boat and exulting in the stillness of the sea. Suddenly, the waters parted, the boat shook furiously, and out poked the heads of two enormous creatures. Terrified, I searched my memory for a label—sea monsters, whales? As the mountainous animals vanished beneath the deep, I realized what they were. Manatees!

When the big mammals surfaced again and peered curiously into our boat, I was stunned by my reaction.

"It's like looking into the face of God," I whispered.

Soon after, there was another surprise. Returning from a business trip, Jef casually mentioned that, on a whim, he had visited St. Patrick's Cathedral to light votive candles in memory of his father and my parents. I was shaken by the sense of some mysterious presence stirring in our lives, something filtering through the hard edges of reason. And I wasn't prepared for my reaction this time either. I wasn't ready for the hot tide of regret that rose in my heart as I realized that I'd never prayed for the repose of my parents' souls.

About a month later, I was lazily perusing my bookshelves when the title of one book seemed to light up. As I pulled the book from the shelf, I remembered buying it years ago but never reading it. It was Thomas Merton's *The Seven Storey Mountain,* which the publisher described as a man's search for faith and peace.

Some impulse led me to curl up on the couch and start reading the book. As I pored over the pages, I was intrigued by Merton's spiritual journey—and touched by the notion that perhaps this book was God's way of drawing me back to faith.

Soon I found myself walking into the sanctuary of a church near our home, falling on my knees, and uttering my first prayer in years.

"Lord, help me to believe," I whispered.

Like the beads on a rosary, one event led to another, and it wasn't long before I'd returned to the sacraments and Jef was received into the Church. Despite the enormous changes in our lives, however, I still clung to shreds of my former skepticism. Claims of mystical experiences and miracles made me squirm.

One Sunday at Mass, our pastor introduced four nuns from India to the congregation. They were the Missionaries of Charity, whom Mother Teresa had sent to Atlanta to open a home for poor women with AIDS. I'd read about Mother Teresa and her belief that we encounter Jesus in the suffering poor, and when the sisters, clad in simple white and blue saris, shyly stood up, a thought flashed through my mind: "This is what I've been searching for."

Shortly after, Jef and I visited the dilapidated house on St. Charles Avenue in midtown Atlanta, where the sisters were living. One little nun showed us around, explaining the litany of renovations needed to transform the dreary house into a home fit for Jesus.

We began spending nearly every Saturday for a year helping the sisters. It was a joy to rise early, pack a thermos of coffee, and join the crew of volunteers who were sanding, painting, and hammering side by side with the sisters.

One day the sisters excitedly told us that Mother Teresa was planning a visit to Atlanta for the consecration of the home. And we were invited.

Jef and I rose before dawn on the day of the Mass. Still, when we arrived at St. Charles Avenue, we saw that a large crowd, plus TV crews, had already gathered outside. What would motivate people, I wondered, to come from all over the city to glimpse this woman? Was it because the media had turned her into a celebrity? What about me? Was I guilty of stargazing too?

Jef and I squeezed through the front door into the living room, where Mass was to be celebrated. But the room already was jammed with people, so we joined the throng in the adjacent dining area, where the air bristled with anticipation. Some people spoke in hushed tones of previous encounters with Mother. Others murmured of miracles.

Miracles, I thought grumpily, don't happen in the 20th century. And, besides, nothing could top my encounter with the manatees.

A commotion near the back door startled me. Whispers darted through the room like fireflies on a summer evening: "Mother is on her way!"

I turned just in time to see a line of nuns, all wearing identical saris, proceeding through the dining room, just a few feet away from us. I realized that the smallest sister was Mother Teresa.

As she passed us, a woman reached out and gently touched the hem of Mother's sari. I imagined what my reaction would have been. Most likely, I thought, I'd have ignored the light touch and continued walking. But Mother Teresa stopped and turned slowly. She smiled at the woman and grasped her outstretched hand.

Then Mother Teresa looked toward me. Our eyes met.

Instantly, I recognized the same light radiating from her eyes that I'd seen in the manatees' eyes. It was as if God had momentarily superimposed one image upon the other.

Until that moment, I'd thought of mystical experiences as technicolor productions, with rumbling skies and luminescent angels brandishing trumpets. And I'd believed that God reserved such grandiose happenings for holy people, certainly not for skeptics like me.

Then I remembered Jesus' words: "I was hungry and you gave me food, I was thirsty and you gave me something to drink, I was a stranger and you welcomed me" (Matthew 25:35).

And I felt that Christ was reminding me to seek Him everywhere. In places untouched by reason but where faith flowers. In the weary faces of the poor, in the compassionate gaze of a saint—and even in the eyes of curious sea creatures.

27

❖ The Turtle ❖

The box turtle was lumbering toward the busy stream of traffic. He seemed unaware that he was inches away from disaster.

Quickly I put on my turn signal, pulled over to the side of the road, and rushed over to retrieve him. Obviously unaware of my kind intentions, the animal took one look at me and vanished into his shell. I carried him carefully to the car and tucked him away in the hatchback.

And then, as I drove home, I felt something stirring in my heart. Something I hadn't felt for quite a while. It was joy.

I was sure the turtle was a gift from God. A lovely outpouring of kindness meant just for me. A touch of grace on a dreary morning.

Not too long ago, I would have dismissed that notion as ridiculous. I didn't believe God tinkered with the tiny events of our everyday lives. When my sister thanked God for finding her a parking space at the mall, I scoffed. When a friend prayed for sunshine for an outdoor wedding, I rolled my eyes.

Surely, I thought, God doesn't meddle in such humdrum affairs. Surely the Big Guy responds only to life's weightier matters. Serious illnesses, job hunts, broken hearts—those sorts of things.

All around me buds were bursting into flowers, blueberries were fattening, and feisty chipmunks were scooting across the yard. It didn't cross my mind that such everyday events might be evidence of God's grace—until my picture of God started changing.

One day, I was with my friend Pam, accompanying her on a trip to retrieve her son, Stephen, from kindergarten. Looking tired and sweaty, the little boy climbed into the car and into his car seat. A few moments later, I heard him whoop for joy as he discovered the surprise. His mom had packed a chilled milk cup and crackers just for him.

That night, I watched Pam put her baby girl, Sarah, to bed. There was the bath and fresh pajamas, of course. But she also made sure the child had her favorite stuffed animals by her side.

This loving mother, I realized, was overseeing the tiniest details in her children's lives to ensure their happiness. Little things like crackers and stuffed animals may seem trivial to us, but they're momentous to a child.

And that's when I concluded that God surely must seek little ways to delight His children. If He's aware of the sparrow falling from the tree, then surely He's in touch with the ebb and flow of our daily lives.

He certainly would have known that on the morning when I rescued the box turtle, my spirits were bedraggled. And He certainly would have known I've been a lifelong fan of turtles, which were my first pets when I was a child.

Love so often is found in the details. You see this clearly in Christ's ministry. When a young couple ran out of wine at a wedding feast, it was no earth-shattering matter, but Christ took pity on them. And surely one lost sheep from a big flock might be dismissed as a trivial matter, but in Christ's eyes, that sheep was worthy of rescue—and its return to the flock was a cause for celebration.

He also unveiled His compassionate heart when He restored a little girl to life while her grieving parents watched. And then He did something rather surprising, but equally kind, when He told the parents to get her something to eat (Mark 5:43). His concern was a small matter, but no doubt it was enormously comforting to the child.

As I released the turtle in our backyard and watched him trotting happily toward the small pond, I had an inkling of how that little girl probably felt. It's nice knowing God is there for you when the big things happen and you really need Him. But sometimes it's the small acts that really count.

28

 Eternal Moments

It's an October evening and we're vacationing on Cedar Key, a small island off the Gulf coast of Florida. We're chasing the sunset in our little boat, the Sea Moose, with a bottle of champagne packed in ice.

As the wind shakes the fabric of the sea, the Sea Moose pitches and bucks precipitously. It doesn't take long to realize Mother Nature's in a decidedly feisty mood this evening and it's best to bow to her whims. So, we return to shore, climb out, and tie off the boat. Then we hurry to our car and head to the marshes, praying we're not too late for the show.

We find a small, deserted dock and settle ourselves comfortably on the edge. But just as Jef is making headway on uncorking the champagne bottle, a herd of gnats descends eagerly upon our flesh. We swat frantically, grab the champagne, exit the dock, and jump back into the car.

It's a very short drive to a ribbon of deserted beach, where we emerge cautiously from the car and perch upon the hood. After murmuring a prayer of thanksgiving—no gnats!—we finally start sipping the champagne. And marveling—for we've found front row seats to tonight's show.

The big bald head of the sun is dipping ever so slowly beneath the horizon. As it moves, the jagged oyster reefs become silhouetted in the orange light, turning black against a now purple sea. In just moments, the sun has vanished, leaving a cardinal red sky painted in bands of amber.

Now the wind stirs voluptuously against the passive sea, which erupts in tiny waves of goose bumps. When the wind retreats momentarily, the water relaxes, seeming to loosen its muscles in a sensual surrender. A few minutes later, long orange fingers of light touch the oyster beds, transforming them to scarlet. A few more minutes and the color of the beds shifts to inky black.

Two glasses of champagne later, with the air growing chilly, we put on jackets and ready ourselves for the second act of the show. It stars a moon floating in the sky like a sand dollar, with a rhinestone star winking nearby.

"Star light, star bright, first star I see tonight," I chant.

"I wish I may, I wish I might." And then I decide to wish for the impossible.

"I want this moment to last forever."

It's the same wish I made as a child once I'd realized that I had the power to tuck away events in my memory. The first time I'd tried this trick, I was in a shoe store with my mother.

In those days, many shoe stores sported X-ray machines, which kids clambered to use. I'm not sure how an X-ray of a child's foot was supposed to help a salesman sell a shoe, but I recall that putting my foot into the machine was as much fun as getting a lollipop from the dentist.

Today, of course, such a casual use of X-rays would be considered horrifying, but then we were blissfully ignorant. It was jolly fun to get a glimpse of your innards. I liked seeing the ghostly white bones in my feet, especially around Halloween when I felt some kinship with trick-or-treat skeletons.

One day, as I was gazing downward at the X-ray of my feet, I thought, "I'll remember this moment forever." And, for better or worse, I have.

Years later, I learned that certain events automatically are stashed in our perpetual memory banks. I'll never forget my mother's pinched and somber face as she lay in her coffin, nor the telephone call from my sister six months later telling me our father had died.

I'll never forget my dear husband's smile as he stood at the altar, awaiting the bride who was slowly making her way up the aisle, her veil trembling in nervousness.

Perhaps this moment tonight beneath the Florida sky would automatically have been stored in my memory. But I don't want to take any chances.

And so I make my wish again: "I want this moment to last forever."

So far, so good. For years to come, whenever I riffle through my shining memories of Cedar Key, I select this one like an especially nice seashell from a collection, turning it over lovingly in my mind's eye. And each time I cherish this magical evening when the sun so graciously surrendered her domain to the moon.

Questions for Reflection and Discussion

1. In what ways is your life filled with grace?

2. In what unlikely places have you encountered God?

3. Was there ever a time when you felt a mysterious sense of "someone" working in your life?

XI

Loving

The morning after my mother died, the woman sharing her hospital room made a mystifying comment to my father.

She said she'd been awakened in the middle of the night by bright lights that had flooded the room. For years the woman's report haunted me. I didn't believe she was simply referring to the overhead lights in the room, but I was puzzled by her words.

Her story reminded me, over and over again, that I hadn't been with my mother on the night she died.

The year was 1976. I had just returned to my apartment in Gainesville, Florida, after celebrating Christmas with my parents in Ft. Lauderdale, when I received a frantic phone call from my father. My mother's condition had suddenly worsened, he told me. Frantic, I packed my bags and rushed to the airport.

When I arrived at the hospital in Ft. Lauderdale, my mother was conscious but weaker than I had ever seen her. Her breathing was labored and she seemed flattened by the pain. Still, she brightened when she saw me, as she always did when I visited. After all, this was a woman who had, for years, kept an extra, fully furnished bedroom in her condo, in case her grown, unmarried daughter might decide to move home permanently. She truly loved me.

As we talked, my mother noticed that I was coughing. When I admitted that I had a sore throat and felt feverish, she looked worried. I tried to make light of my illness because I wanted to stay with her in the hospital that night, but my mother wouldn't hear of it. Instead, she insisted that my father take me back to the condo.

"Make sure she gets plenty of sleep," she whispered.

My father and I bowed to her motherly wisdom. As darkness fell, we kissed my mother goodbye and returned to the condo, where I downed several aspirin and soon fell asleep.

The next morning, I was awakened very early by the sound of the front door opening. It was still dark outside. As I struggled to wake up, I realized my father was returning from an early-morning visit to the hospital.

One look at his face and I knew. My mother had died during the night.

Even though I'd had years to prepare myself emotionally for her death, I was shattered. It was impossible to imagine my life without her. Sobbing, I collapsed on the couch.

My father, weeping too, told me how peaceful my mother had looked that morning. And it was then he mentioned her roommate's report about the lights.

Wracked with grief and remorse, I didn't comment. Even though my mother had encouraged me to go home that night, I blamed myself for not insisting on staying. I felt I had failed my mother on the most momentous night of her life.

Many years later, while I was reading the account of Christ's passion, the waves of anguish and self-recrimination started to recede. As I began looking at my mother's death through a new lens, I started freeing myself from the clutches of remorse that had gripped me for so long.

I was deeply impressed by Christ's enormous gesture of compassion to the thief dying beside Him on the cross. Despite His own terrible suffering, Christ had wanted to comfort the man. And He did so by uttering the words: "Today you will be with me in Paradise" (Luke 23:43).

As I began revisiting my memory of my last encounter with my mother, I realized that, in her own way, she had been radiating Christ's tender love. Despite her suffering, she had heeded the gentle impulses of her heart by encouraging me to get a good night's sleep.

I think I've finally grasped the significance of her roommate's report. It is just conjecture, of course, since I wasn't there, but I believe the woman was conveying a very important message to my father and me.

I believe she was telling the truth about seeing bright lights that night. And I believe they were angels. Coming to escort my beloved mother home.

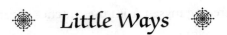

29

Little Ways

It was a dreadful day. I was having a serious attack of the "poor me" syndrome.

"Poor me, I'm ill. Poor me, my life is a mess. Poor me, I'm suffering."

Pam hugged me wordlessly as I poured out my tribulations on her shoulder. Her daughter—my goddaughter, Sarah, 2—perched nearby on the couch, studying us both.

Suddenly Sarah rose from the couch and tottered across the floor in my direction. She wrapped her plump arms around me and planted a kiss on my knees. I started giggling through my tears.

Sometimes we forget such tiny gestures can be treasures. We throw an elaborate shindig for our toddler's birthday—clowns prancing on the lawn, a blown-up funhouse—when the kids might be content playing pin-the-tail-on-the-donkey.

At Christmas especially, we may be tempted to think in grandiose ways. It's easy to believe that the more gifts we buy, the better. The bigger the tree, the better. And that same mentality can haunt our charitable impulses.

We start believing we can never do enough for others.

Maybe you're working ten-hour days and when Saturdays roll around, you're exhausted. Instead of pitching in at the church bake sale, you whip up brownies for your husband. Then you feel guilty. You figure that when you die, the gates of heaven will be padlocked.

But there may be another key that will open those gates. It's not glittering or ornate—and it rarely makes headlines.

It is the little way of love, which St. Thérèse of Lisieux wrote about in her autobiography, *Story of a Soul*. In 1888, at the tender age of 15, St. Thérèse entered a Carmelite convent. Stricken with tuberculosis, she died nine years later. In her short life, she took seriously Christ's invitation about "letting the little children come to me."

Children can't perform great deeds, she realized, but they can show great love. So she perfected a childlike love, "a little way to heaven, very short and direct."

"My little way is the way of spiritual childhood, the way of trust and absolute self-surrender," she wrote.

We glimpse the heart of selfless love when Christ reminds His disciples that God hides in unexpected places—in strangers, in prisoners, in the hungry, and the ailing.

The stranger may be the new guy at work. The prisoner may be a neighbor who is housebound after surgery. The hungry one may be a kid dipping a hand in the cookie jar.

Small gestures can splash light in a desert of darkness. Perhaps you're out walking and you see someone heading in your direction. You have a choice. You can pretend to be studying your shoelaces and ignore the person—or you can beam them a smile.

The gospels overflow with simple showings of love. There's the poor woman who gives her last coin to help others. And the woman who anoints the Lord's feet with her tears. A humble gesture, but it seems to deeply touch His heart.

Mother Teresa, who embraced the little way of St. Thérèse, began her ministry by rescuing one dying person from a road in India. That was only a drop in the ocean when you consider the millions of people who were suffering. One kindness led to another, and eventually Mother Teresa created a sea of love. She always advised that we do small things with great love.

At Christmas, that small thing might be visiting a lonely neighbor. Baking a child's favorite cookies. Or, if you happen to be two years old, planting a smooch on your godmother's knees when she's got a serious case of the blues.

30

 Trio of Love Notes

I was a melancholy child. The photo albums show a toddler with a woebegone expression peeking at the world between the bars of a playpen.

My earliest memory is trailing my mom around the house as she vacuumed and asking her over and over, "Do you love me?" Silencing the roaring machine momentarily, she'd reply, "Of course I do."

But some kids never really believe that. Especially if you were one of the misfits, too pudgy or too tall, too scrawny or too brainy.

I was one of the fat kids. Much to my horror, the neighborhood kids dubbed me "Fatty," a nickname that trailed me into elementary school, where there was also a tall, skinny girl ("String Bean"), a little boy with thick glasses ("Four Eyes"), and a child who lived in poverty and didn't bathe regularly ("Stinky").

When Sister assured the class that God loved us, I was skeptical. Why would He love someone who didn't fit in? Someone the other kids delighted in taunting? Someone who was always among the last chosen for the softball team?

After a ferocious bout of dieting in my twenties, I finally slimmed down, and today people marvel when I confide that I was once overweight and dumpy. Still, once you've been a misfit, that mentality haunts you all your life. At times your self-esteem seems lower than a snake's belly. You have a hard time believing anyone could really care about you.

One night recently I was struggling with a fierce case of the blues. Suddenly I felt as if I'd been thrust back in time to my first-grade classroom, surrounded by the jeering faces of my classmates. I was the fat kid again, lonely and despised. I sat on the couch and wept mightily.

"No one loves me," I roared, "not even God."

The next morning, I checked my e-mail to discover that a dear friend had sent me a note brimming with affection. Tears came to my eyes as I read her message.

"You are my dearest and best friend, my sister, and life is better because of you," Pam wrote. "You bring great joy to my life . . . and I love you very much."

I marveled at the timeliness of her message. There was no way she could have known about my distress the night before. What a coincidence, I thought—until suddenly I remembered Carl Jung's theory of synchronicity. Dismissing coincidences, he cautioned us instead to heed events that seem inexplicably connected in our daily lives. They might contain messages we need to hear.

The next day, when I returned home from work, I saw the light pulsing on my phone-answering machine. Listening to the recording, I felt a chill race up and down my spine. The caller was a woman I'd never met, someone who had read my articles in *The Atlanta Journal-Constitution*. She said she'd been moved by the Holy Spirit to contact me.

"I want you to know what a blessing you've been to me," she said. "I don't know where you are on your spiritual journey, but I want to encourage you and assure you I'm praying for you."

I was stunned. In some mysterious way, these two stirring proclamations of affection and support seemed made-to-order responses to my earlier outburst of despair.

The next morning, I was riding the shuttle bus from the parking deck to the library where I work. After the other passengers had departed, I struck up a conversation with the driver, a heavy-set black woman in her forties. She told me how much she loved driving the little bus. Even though some folks might grow bored driving the same circular route for hours, she said she enjoyed praying—and singing—when she was alone on the bus.

"What do you like to sing?" I asked her.

"Oh, just different things," she said, suddenly shy.

Then, as she navigated the bus over a speed bump, she glanced at me in the rear view mirror and beamed me a big smile.

Seconds later, she belted out, "Jesus loves me, this I know because the Bible tells me so."

I found myself marveling as I departed the shuttle. Maybe I might have shrugged off the first two events as mere coincidences, but this third one wouldn't easily bow its head to the sword of reason. Something mysterious was going on here.

And then I remembered the one who embraced the lepers, the prostitutes, the broken-down, and the despondent. The one who was stripped and beaten. And taunted by the crowd.

"OK, my dearest Jesus," I whispered in prayer, "I get it. You're telling me you love me. And you're reminding me you never give up on anyone. Not even the misfits."

31

A Valentine for God

The glow of Valentine's Day cards displayed in a card shop can illuminate the dreariest winter day. There are fancy concoctions for your sweetheart, your parents, your kids, and your friends.

This year, as I was reading the fierce inscriptions of love and friendship, I found myself daydreaming. I wondered what it might be like to send a valentine to God.

That notion would have unsettled me when I was a kid. That's because I prayed to a rather distant old man perched on a heavenly throne. Sadly, His love had strings attached. If you cleaned your room, you deserved His affection, but if you failed a spelling test, He turned His back on you. And He was certainly too busy overseeing the universe to read a love note from a child.

All these years later, I'm trying to embrace a different version of our Heavenly Father. I'm longing to know the God of unconditional love, whom St. John described when he wrote, "Beloved, let us love one another because love is from God" (1 John 4:7).

No matter how blue, broken, or weary you may be, it seems unconditional love can boost you through another day. Even if you burn the supper and wreck the car, somehow you know things will turn out fine. You won't be kicked off the team.

Marriage vows are written in the ink of unconditional love. We promise to stay with our spouse through thick or thin.

"For richer or poorer, in sickness and in health," we chant somewhat naively when we're young and robust and on the fast track to success.

As the years pass, sometimes we're tempted to edit the vows. "I'll stay with you if you get a promotion." Or: "I'll stay with you if you lose 20 pounds."

In our world today, unconditional love seems in short supply. Wherever we turn, we must jump through hoops to get approval. The boss demands we meet a quota. Our neighbors expect a well-manicured yard. The kids are clamoring for a trip to the beach.

What a relief it is to realize that Christ's love has no strings attached.

He kept company with prostitutes, lepers, beggars, and thieves, an unsavory crowd who shared one thing in common. They longed to be loved, just as they were. In their poverty, illness or sinfulness. And He didn't disappoint them.

Still, it's hard to believe Christ needed their affection. It's hard to imagine a lion needing anything from an ant. But the gospels say otherwise, especially in one telling scene where Christ asks Peter three times, "Do you love me?" (John 21:15-17).

I believe He repeated the question because His friend's love mattered to Him—just as ours does.

Valentine's Day seems a fine time to tell Him of our love. A fine time to send the Lord a valentine carved from the pain and joy of our ordinary lives. It may be streaked with a mother's tears and creased by a father's weariness. Maybe the baby chewed the edges off. Maybe the dog slept on it.

But I believe Christ will accept our tattered valentines with joy. I trust He will *ooh* and *ah* like a mom exclaiming over a baby's sincere attempts at drawing an elephant. And I hope He'll appreciate our heartfelt sentiments.

"Dear Jesus: It's me. The one who sometimes stumbles on the path of faith. The one who sometimes falls off cliffs. For whatever it's worth, I give you my heart. No strings attached."

Questions for Reflection and Discussion

1. Reflect on the past week. Has God sent you any little "love notes"?

2. Describe your childhood image(s) of God the Father and Christ the Son. Are your feelings about God different today?

3. What are some little ways of showing others that you love them?

Bibliography

Autobiography of Saint Thérèse of Lisieux. Translated by John Beevers. New York: Doubleday, 1989.

The Catholic Prayer Book. Compiled by Msgr. Michael Buckley. Ann Arbor: Servant Books, 1986.

Catholic Women's Devotional Bible. Grand Rapids, MI: Zondervan Publishing Company, 2000.

DeMello, Anthony. *The Song of the Bird*. New York: Doubleday, 1984.

Dominguez, Joe and Robin, Vicki. *Your Money or Your Life*. New York: Penguin, 1992.

Julian of Norwich. *Revelations of Divine Love*. London: Penguin, 1998.

Keating, Thomas. *Intimacy with God*. New York: Crossroads Publishing Company, 1999.

Merton, Thomas. *The Seven Storey Mountain*. New York: Harcourt Brace Jovanovich, 1976.

Mother Teresa. *No Greater Love*. Novato, California: New World Library, 1997.

Mother Teresa. *Heart of Joy*. Ann Arbor: Servant Books, 1987.

Nouwen, Henri J.M. *The Inner Voice of Love*. New York: Doubleday, 1998.

Rawlings, Marjorie Kinnan. *Cross Creek*. New York: Macmillan Publishing Company, 1970.

Rohr, Richard. *Everything Belongs.* New York: Crossroad Publishing Company, 1999.

Rohr, Richard. *Job and the Mystery of Suffering.* New York: Crossroad Publishing Company, 1998.

St. Benedict's Rule for Monasteries. Translated by Leonard J. Doyle. Collegeville, MN: Liturgical Press, 1948.

Additional Titles Published by Resurrection Press, a Catholic Book Publishing Imprint

A Rachel Rosary *Larry Kupferman*	$4.50
Blessings All Around *Dolores Leckey*	$8.95
Catholic Is Wonderful *Mitch Finley*	$4.95
Come, Celebrate Jesus! *Francis X. Gaeta*	$4.95
Days of Intense Emotion *Keeler/Moses*	$12.95
From Holy Hour to Happy Hour *Francis X. Gaeta*	$7.95
Healing through the Mass *Robert DeGrandis, SSJ*	$9.95
Our Grounds for Hope *Fulton J. Sheen*	$7.95
The Healing Rosary *Mike D.*	$5.95
Healing Your Grief *Ruthann Williams, OP*	$7.95
Heart Peace *Adolfo Quezada*	$9.95
Life, Love and Laughter *Jim Vlaun*	$7.95
Living Each Day by the Power of Faith *Barbara Ryan*	$8.95
The Joy of Being a Catechist *Gloria Durka*	$4.95
The Joy of Being a Eucharistic Minister *Mitch Finley*	$5.95
The Joy of Being a Lector *Mitch Finley*	$5.95
The Joy of Marriage Preparation *McDonough/Marinelli*	$5.95
The Joy of Music Ministry *J.M. Talbot*	$6.95
The Joy of Preaching *Rod Damico*	$6.95
The Joy of Being an Usher *Gretchen Hailer, RSHM*	$5.95
Lights in the Darkness *Ave Clark, O.P.*	$8.95
Loving Yourself for God's Sake *Adolfo Quezada*	$5.95
Mother Teresa *Eugene Palumbo, S.D.B.*	$5.95
Personally Speaking *Jim Lisante*	$8.95
Practicing the Prayer of Presence *Muto/van Kaam*	$8.95
Prayers from a Seasoned Heart *Joanne Decker*	$8.95
Praying the Lord's Prayer with Mary *Muto/vanKaam*	$8.95
5-Minute Miracles *Linda Schubert*	$4.95
Season of New Beginnings *Mitch Finley*	$4.95
Season of Promises *Mitch Finley*	$4.95
Soup Pot *Ethel Pochocki*	$8.95
Stay with Us *John Mullin, SJ*	$3.95
Surprising Mary *Mitch Finley*	$7.95
Teaching as Eucharist *Joanmarie Smith*	$5.95
What He Did for Love *Francis X. Gaeta*	$5.95
Woman Soul *Pat Duffy, OP*	$7.95
You Are My Beloved *Mitch Finley*	$10.95
Your Sacred Story *Robert Lauder*	$6.95

For a free catalog call 1-800-892-6657